Factoring
and
Invoice
Discounting

A Guide to
Factoring
and
Invoice
Discounting
The new bankers

Tim Lea
Cashflow Solutions Ltd
Brighton, UK

Wendy Trollope
The PR Company
Brighton, UK

CHAPMAN & HALL
London · Glasgow · Weinheim · New York · Tokyo · Melbourne · Madras

Published by Chapman & Hall, 2–6 Boundary Row, London SE1 8HN, UK

Chapman & Hall, 2–6 Boundary Row, London SE1 8HN, UK

Blackie Academic & Professional, Wester Cleddens Road, Bishopbriggs, Glasgow G64 2NZ, UK

Chapman & Hall GmbH, Pappelallee 3, 69469 Weinheim, Germany

Chapman & Hall USA, 115 Fifth Avenue, New York, NY 10003, USA

Chapman & Hall Japan, ITP-Japan, Kyowa Building, 3F, 2-2-1 Hirakawacho, Chiyoda-ku, Tokyo 102, Japan

Chapman & Hall Australia, 102 Dodds Street, South Melbourne, Victoria 3205, Australia

Chapman & Hall India, R. Seshadri, 32 Second Main Road, CIT East, Madras 600 035, India

First edition 1996

© 1996 Tim Lea and Wendy Trollope

Typeset in 10/12pt Méridien by Saxon Graphics Ltd, Derby
Printed in Great Britain by St Edmundsbury Press, Bury St Edmunds, Suffolk

ISBN 0 412 61370 0

A catalogue record for this book is available from the British Library

Library of Congress Catalog Card Number: 95-78845

∞ Printed on permanent acid-free text paper, manufactured in accordance with ANSI/NISO Z39.48-1992 and ANSI/NISO Z39.48-1984 (Permanence of Paper).

Contents

Foreword

The Rt. Hon. the Earl Ferrers
Minister for Small Firms and
Consumer Affairs

Small firms play an important role in the growth and the prosperity of the economy. To fulfil their potential in increasingly competitive markets, they need to have access to advice and information on all the services which are available to help them. This is particularly important when firms are considering alternative sources of finance.

I therefore welcome all initiatives, such as this guide, which increase awareness of the options which are available and which provide information to help firms to assess which facilities are most appropriate to their needs.

Preface

AIMS

The demand for factoring and invoice discounting services has grown steadily and with the current economic conditions stands to expand even faster.

From our research, awareness of the variety of services on offer to UK businesses is poor. Business people and financial advisors will gain from a better understanding and we have sought to share our knowledge with them. Around 250 000 firms in the UK could benefit from these services but only around 12 000 use them. From our experience within the industry and latterly as independent consultants we are able to give the reader inside information, previously unpublished, about the way the industry works. We give practical tips on eligibility, how to negotiate best rates, avoid rejection by the factor and save money. There are contact details of around 40 factors and discounters and help with where to get best advice. This book is designed to help advisors do a better job for clients and help small- and medium-sized businesses assess for themselves exactly what factoring and invoice discounting can do for them.

While looking in detail at the UK market we also examine advances made in the USA that are likely to influence the industry in the near future.

We emphasise that factoring and discounting are no longer the 'poor relations' of traditional banking, and give due recognition for the skills and services that are suited to companies in the 1990s. Ours is the first book to suggest that the factor could have the same importance as the banker in financing small- and medium-sized businesses. As property values remain relatively weak, the sales ledger has in many cases become the main asset. Companies must therefore make use of the sales ledger to generate maximum cash.

Independent factors and discounters are also given a voice – their valuable services have hitherto been largely overlooked.

In conclusion, however, we have not shied away from areas where the industry can improve its services and its approach to finance professionals and businesses.

Acknowledgements

We were given a great deal of assistance with the writing of this book and would particularly like to thank Mark Spofforth, Vice-Chairman of the General Practitioner Board of the ICAEW and Robin Ebers, Deputy Director-General of the Institute of Export for taking part in interviews. Our thanks also to BDO Binder Hamlyn for their views on the first draft and to our editor Sarah Henderson.

Thanks also to the following:

Aubrey Selig, Association of Invoice Factors
The Association of British Factors & Discounters
Roger De B Hovell, Debtco
Paul Samrah, Kingston Smith Chartered Accountants
Paul Dawson, Jardine Credit Insurance Ltd
Barclays Commercial Services Ltd
Ian Stuttard, Barclays Bank plc
Roger White, Midland Bank plc
David Kilburn, Lombard NatWest Commercial Services Ltd
Pat Munday, Maddox Factoring (UK) Ltd
TSB
Factors Chain International
David Marsden, RDM Factors Limited
John Chesterfield, Alex Lawrie Factors.

Chapter 1

The UK factoring market

AN OVERVIEW OF THE MARKET

The UK factoring market began in earnest in the early 1960s and has since developed into a £22bn industry. The UK market currently comprises around 62 factoring and trade finance houses, providing factoring, invoice discounting and 'merchant' financing services to around 12 000 companies in the UK.

The marketplace has two established trade associations, the Association of British Factors and Discounters (ABF&D) and the Association of Invoice Factors (AIF). Both lay down financial criteria for their members and operate within strict codes of conduct.

The ABF&D comprises 12 of the major factoring companies, and is estimated to occupy some 90% of the marketplace, whilst the Association of Invoice Factors has 9 active members, each being smaller independent factoring companies, occupying around 1.6% of the overall market. The remaining market share comprises a number of independent factoring and invoice discounting houses, which for a variety of reasons have not sought to join the associations.

MARKET STRUCTURE

The majority of the factoring and invoice discounting houses are backed by financial institutions, although many of the smaller independent factoring companies are privately backed, using external finance.

As Table 1.1 demonstrates, the market continues to be dominated by the five high street banks, with around 63% of the market controlled by the banks of Lloyds, National Westminster, Barclays, Midland and TSB. Equally, Lloyds Bank has in excess of 27% of the overall market through their two subsidiaries, International Factors Ltd and Alex Lawrie Factors Ltd.

Table 1.1   Adjusted market share of the ABF&D members 1993

	Shareholders	Total volume of business (£m)	Total adjusted market share[1] (%)
International Factors Ltd	Lloyds Bank plc – 100%	3917	17.72
Lombard Natwest Commercial Services Ltd	National Westminster Bank Group – 100%	3361	15.21
Griffin Factors Ltd	Midland Bank plc – 100%	3076	13.92
Alex Lawrie Factors Ltd	Lloyds Bank plc – 100%	2138	9.67
TSB Commercial Finance Ltd	TSB Group plc	1500	6.79
Barclays Commercial Services Ltd	Barclays Bank plc – 100%	1398	6.33
Royal Bank Invoice Finance Ltd	The Royal Bank of Scotland plc – 100%	1098	4.97
Trade Indemnity–Heller Commercial Finance Ltd	Trade Indemnity Group plc – 50% Heller Europe Ltd[2] – 50%	1082	4.90
Kellock Ltd	Bank of Scotland 97.5% Management 2.5%	987	4.47
UCB Discounting Ltd	UCB Group plc – 100%	703	3.18
Close Invoice Finance Ltd	Close Brothers Group plc – 95% Management – 5%	327	1.48
Venture Factors Ltd	ABN AMRO Group	304	1.38
Total ABF&D		19 891	90
Total estimated market		2210	

Source: ABF&D annual report 1993.[3]

[1] Adjusted to take into account the fact that ABF&D has 90% of market share.

[2] Heller Europe is ultimately owned by The Fuji Bank Ltd.

[3] At the time of writing, September 1994, six-monthly figures have been released for the ABF&D which highlighted continued growth for the period January–June 1994. For the six-month period an increase of 19% on turnover was seen.

MARKET PERFORMANCE

The performance of the market, as determined by the levels of client turnover shown in Table 1.2, confirms solid underlying strength, with continued growth being seen. Over the period 1982–1993, the market saw annual compound growth in excess of 20%.

Table 1.2 Combined business volumes of ABF&D members 1982–1993

	Combined business levels (£bn)	Overall market growth	
		1982=100	%
1982	2.6	100	
1983	2.7	103.85	3.85
1984	3.5	134.62	29.63
1985	4.3	165.38	22.86
1986	5.2	200	20.93
1987	7.0	269.23	34.62
1988	8.5	326.92	21.43
1989	10.4	400	22.35
1990	13.3	511.54	27.88
1991	13.6	523.08	2.26
1992	15.97	614.25	17.43
1993	19.7	757.37	23.3
	Average annual growth		20.17%

Source: ABF&D.

The underlying strength of the marketplace is based on a combination of external and internal forces. Firstly, from an external point of view, companies and their financial advisors are increasingly recognising the greater flexibility of factoring and invoice discounting compared to the traditional bank overdraft. This trend has steadily been reinforced by the banks' general inability to support growing companies' increased demand for finance, owing to the increased working capital requirement outstripping the banks' traditional level of security in many situations. Secondly, internally, the major high street banks, who ultimately control the majority of the marketplace, have been heavily marketing their respective in-house factoring and invoice discounting arms through to their existing clients.

For the banks, both forms of finance represent a more secure means of advancing increased funds, whilst generating higher returns on capital employed. The 'supply-push' effect has led to substantial enquiry levels for the high-street backed factors, with 50–80% of their business coming from their parent banks.

Equally, the belief that factoring companies are recession-proof appears to be unfounded. During the middle of the 1990–1992 recession, the underlying growth of the marketplace faltered markedly to just over 2% in the year ending December 1992, a fall in real terms. Whilst banks' resistance to lending during recessionary times would lead companies to look for other forms of finance, increasing the enquiry levels for factoring, recession did not stimulate growth for the market as a whole. The downturn in the levels of factored turnover during the 1990–1992 recession was seen as a result of the following:

- Weakened economic conditions restricted commercial growth opportunities, not only directly reducing demand for growth-led finance, but also reducing the factors' existing clients' turnover.
- Whilst the level of new business enquiry was high as a result of the banks' reluctance to lend, the volume of business actually taken on was lower as the factors sought to be increasingly cautious, after frauds, bad debts and a number of factoring companies exiting the marketplace took their toll upon confidence.
- Recession generates a culture of corporate failure. A number of the factors' clients failed during this period, resulting in an immediate loss in market turnover.

MARKET PERFORMANCE BY PRODUCT

The ABF&D statistics in respect of the key products – factoring and invoice discounting – show how the structural emphasis of the marketplace has swung towards invoice discounting. Marked growth has been experienced in this sector, with 28% compound growth seen as compared to 13% for factoring for the period 1982–1993 (Table 1.3).

Table 1.3 The growth of factoring and invoice discounting by ABF&D members 1982–1993

Year	Domestic factoring growth			Invoice discounting growth		
	£bn	1982 = 100	% growth	£bn	1982 = 100	% growth
1982	1.7	100		0.9	100	
1983	1.9	111.76	11.76	0.8	88.89	−11.11
1984	2.3	135.29	21.05	1.2	133.33	50.00
1985	2.7	158.82	17.39	1.6	177.78	33.33
1986	3.0	176.47	11.11	2.2	244.44	37.50
1987	3.8	223.53	26.67	3.2	355.56	45.45
1988	4.5	264.71	18.42	4.0	444.44	25.00
1989	4.9	288.24	8.89	5.5	611.11	37.50
1990	5.3	311.76	8.16	8.0	888.89	45.45
1991	5.2	305.88	−1.89	8.4	933.33	5.00
1992	5.6	328.82	7.50	9.7	1079.76	15.69
1993	6.5	382.35	16.28	12.4	1377.78	27.60
Average growth over the period			13.21%			28.31%

Source: ABF&D annual report 1993.

Whilst factoring has become the backbone of the industry, invoice discounting is increasing in popularity, as a result of an underlying structural shift in companies' needs:

- Technology has improved substantially over the period, with the advent of computerisation and effective simple accounting packages heralding the reduced need for sales ledger administration, one of the key services historically provided by the full service factoring.

- Invoice discounting provides the financial benefits of factoring whilst enabling client companies to maintain complete control of their relationships with their customers, and in certain circumstances offering the opportunity for their customers to be totally unaware of the factoring company's involvement.
- Many larger companies have recognised the benefits of financing growth through sales-linked finance. However, good financial controls developed over their corporate life span have minimised the need for third-party administrative assistance.
- In some quarters the historic stigma associated with disclosed factoring is still prevalent, with many companies favouring non-disclosure of the facility.

International factoring facilities represent a very small part of the marketplace, and are provided by around 12 factoring companies. Within the ABF&D, international factoring represents only about 3.8% of the marketplace, approximately £0.76bn of client turnover (Table 1.4).

Table 1.4 ABF&D members' volumes of business to 31.12.93

Market sector	Volume of business (£bn)	%
Domestic factoring	6.51	33.1
Invoice discounting	12.4	63.1
International factoring	0.76	3.8

Source: ABF&D annual report 1993.

Although growth in the provision of international factoring services was up by 18% over the previous year, it still represents a small area of the marketplace. In part, because of the increased costs in providing export facilities, it has not been as sufficiently profitable for many factors to pursue this market sector. However, with the exit of many banks from the provision of credit insurance supported export finance, the way may be paved to develop this marketplace more effectively. Indeed in recent years some of the factoring companies have developed sales roles dedicated to the pursuit of export factoring facilities.

AVERAGE CLIENT SIZE

Across the members of the ABF&D, the average client size has grown to approximately £1.95m. Factoring clients average just over £1m, and the average invoice discounting client, £4.45m.

The AIF average client size is considerably smaller by comparison to the ABF&D members, primarily because their members typically target the smaller end of the market (Table 1.5).

Table 1.5   The average client size by turnover by trade association, 1993

	ABF&D	AIF
Factoring	c £1m	£459 000
Invoice discounting	£4.45m	n/a

Source: ABF&D and AIF.

Figure 1.1 shows the breakdown of the ABF&D clients by turnover. The bulk of clients who factor (about 80%) are of the range up to £2m turnover. The smaller end of the market, not surprisingly, takes up the bulk of the factors' activity as this represents the key area of business growth – after all, it is easier for a company to double its turnover from £250k to £500k than one doubling from £2m to £4m.

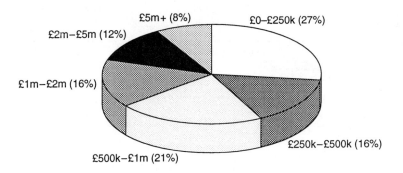

Figure 1.1   The distribution of clients by turnover – ABF&D members 1993 (*source:* ABF&D 1993)

Interestingly, the number of clients with a turnover of below £250k fell by almost 10% over the previous year, indicating the effect of weaker economic conditions reducing the number of new start companies. The key turnover bracket demonstrating interest in factoring facilities are those companies of the range £500k–£1m. As the economic conditions began to improve, so the smaller companies with some track record would have had the flexibility and speed to capitalise upon the increasing sales opportunities.

CREDIT CONTROL AND BAD DEBT EXPERIENCE

The average number of days to collect their clients' invoices (debt turn), among the ABF&D members stood at a highly creditable 59 days for the year ending 1993. This demonstrated an improved performance on the year ending 1992 (62 days). With various sources of data suggesting the industry average debt turn performance varying between 69 and 84 days, the ABF&D members appear to outperform standard industry criteria by 14–30%.

From a bad debt point of view, eight of the ABF&D members have the ability to provide bad debt protection. On behalf of their clients, ABF&D members absorbed £9.9m of bad debts in the year ending 1993.

INDUSTRY SECTORS OF ACTIVITY

As we will see in later chapters, because of the nature of the services offered by the factoring companies, certain sectors of industry cannot be handled effectively. Typically, those products or services which are 'buy, sell and forget', for example temporary recruitment agencies and light engineering companies, can be factored. The construction industry on the other hand is particularly difficult for the factoring industry to support, although certain areas of activity can be handled, such as plant hire companies. Figure 1.2 shows a breakdown of ABF&D clients by industry sector.

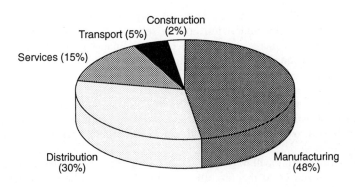

Figure 1.2 Client sectors – ABF&D members 1993 (*source:* ABF&D 1993)

SUPPLEMENTARY INFORMATION – 1994 STATISTICS

Information from the Association of British Factors and Discounters regarding the year ending 31.12.94 highlights that during the time of economic growth for the UK economy the overall turnover factored with the ABFD members increased by 24% to £24.4bn. In volume terms, invoice discounting continued to grow ahead of factoring services, again dominating the industry and representing almost 65% of the marketplace. Record profits have also been returned by many of the leading players within the market, reflective of the positive market conditions prevailing during the year.

Table 1.6 Factoring market statistics 1994

	1993 £m	% of total turnover	1994 £m	% of total turnover	% increase on 1993
Domestic Factoring	£6 514	33.09%	£7 789	31.91%	19.58%
International Factoring	£759	3.86%	£843	3.45%	11.07%
Invoice Discounting	£12 411	63.05%	£15 776	64.63%	27.12%
Total Turnover	£19 683	100.00%	£24 409	100.00%	24.01%

Source: Annual Report ABFD 1994.

Summary

Factoring and invoice discounting facilities continue to be used increasingly, as is reflected in the healthy underlying growth seen in the market. The facilities appear to be gaining increased acceptance within financial circles as a flexible financial tool that can provide an alternative commercial solution to a company's working capital need.

With the increase in computerisation, the shift in market structure away from factoring and towards invoice discounting is not surprising. The ease of access to accounting software packages in particular dispenses with the need for third-party administrative assistance, which has been the historic backbone of the factoring service.

Full service factoring will however continue to cater for companies in the range of up to £1m turnover. At this level most companies will not have sufficient volumes of business to justify the requirement for a full-time credit controller, and so they can benefit from professional third-party backup.

Overall, the marketplace as a whole is likely to continue this pattern of healthy growth as more of the key influencers of financial opinion begin to promote the benefits of the facilities. On a wider level, we are likely to see a sea change in the medium term towards working capital financing in general. The restrictions, the uncertainty and the underlying weakness of the overdraft, together with its repayment on demand, will continue to encourage a structural shift towards factoring and invoice discounting as facilities, with the bankers' role changing to that of supplying longer-term finance and other financial products.

Chapter 2

Factoring and the economic cycle

The economic cycle like all areas of industry determines the attitudes towards risk. Within the financial services arena, the attitude towards risk will determine the levels of finance provision. In this chapter we hope to establish that the factoring and invoice discounting industries are commercial finance solutions for all seasons.

The dynamics of the factoring industry place it in the privileged position of experiencing good enquiry levels whatever the economic conditions. While this may imply that it is resistant to recession, the industry thrives upon its clients' successes. If a client company succeeds so does its factor – after all the factor's fee structure is based upon the level of client sales. If a client fails, however, the factor loses their direct income from that client and is exposed to the potential of bad debt in seeking to recoup their funds. So although recession can improve enquiry levels, it can present a 'double-edged sword' from an income point of view.

FACTORING AND THE RECESSION

Recession results in weakened trading conditions for the corporate sector as a whole. Deteriorating market conditions lead to firms consolidating and resorting to survival strategies as earnings begin to suffer. Consumer confidence is dampened by rounds of job losses, which duly reinforce a downward spiral in the economy and business confidence. This all results in a rise in the level of corporate failures, which in turn generates the culture of 'the credit squeeze'. Interest rates rise, sharply increasing the costs of borrowing, which when considered together with falling income levels further increases the chances of corporate failure. With tight credit, banks and suppliers alike seek to 'batten down the hatches' in order to prepare themselves for the ensuing battle for survival. Investment profiles and strategies become short-term and cash becomes 'king'.

With the requirement to generate cash a priority, internal sources of working capital become the centre of corporate attention. Stocking levels are cut, trade creditors are squeezed, and customers are chased more vigorously. All three together squeeze out precious cash flow.

However, lack of commercial power inhibits the ability of many small businesses to generate additional cash flow from internal sources. Their customers may react adversely to their smaller suppliers seeking earlier payment, while their major suppliers are likely to be larger than themselves and unlikely to offer extended payment terms. This weakened commercial power worsens cash flow, creating a working capital gap which needs to be filled.

In an easier credit environment, the banking sector would hope to fill this void. However, falling asset values together with a tight credit regime restrict the banks' ability to provide additional support. In difficult times, the easiest decision for a bank to make is to say 'no' to additional working capital requirements.

It is the commercial financial institutions who will assess each case in more depth and be in the best position to say 'yes'.

FACTORING – LAST RESORT FINANCE OR 'COMMERCIAL' FINANCE?

Many business people and financial advisors have historically stigmatised factoring as 'last resort finance', a view which has been held by many since the early 1970s. Their view is that factoring is the last ditch attempt to save a company before it goes into liquidation, with their views substantiated by saying '...of course they were factoring before they went bust!'

It is understandable where this view has originated. By virtue of the fact that factoring, in whatever form it is marketed, is borrowing; a company's financial structure is automatically potentially destabilised by taking on board the facility. At a time of recession, higher interest rates will increase the pressure on the serviceability of the increased borrowings, thus directly increasing the chances of failure. Equally, factors will venture into companies where bankers have feared to tread. So by virtue of the bank saying no, the factor's clients will be perceived to be riskier.

However, factors will not just support a company's cash flow by 'pawnbroking' a client's debtor book to generate a short-term high level of return. Whilst pawnbrokers have their role to play, and indeed there are a number of 'non-status' peripheral factoring companies who undertake just this role, the majority of factoring companies want to establish relationships which provide them with long-term income flows and their clients the means with which to finance their sales ambitions.

There is little point in a factor supporting a company in severe difficulties with no chance of being turned around. Doing so just defers the day of judgement. Indeed the upfront expense of generating new business, the costs of realising their security upon a client's insolvency and the increased dangers of fraudulent activity lead to factoring companies only supporting a company where they believe in its underlying viability.

Factors do, however, take a 'commercial view' of business, looking at how their support will add to the success of their potential client. They will critically analyse the company's cash flow and budgetary projections against the background of their client's market sector. Once the business is considered viable, providing the underlying security is satisfactory, the company should be supported. It is the commercial skills of the factoring companies that enable them to assess the viability of the underlying business, and to place an effective value on their security, enabling them to provide finance even in sometimes marginal cases.

In certain cases, for example, where the bank may not be providing support to a business, the factors can provide sufficient support to enable 'credit repair' to be undertaken. In other words, if there are underlying weaknesses which have been recognised by the company's management, factoring and invoice discounting can buy them time to sort out the underlying difficulties and to trade out of their problems.

Sometimes, however, the factors will get it wrong – after all, that is what risk is all about, and they are in 'the risk business'. In most cases, however, they will get it right resulting in ongoing profitable clients.

Thus, factors can be viewed as 'commercial financiers' taking an overall view of the business and its risks, providing support to the companies they believe will succeed.

RECESSION TO RECOVERY

Recessions batter balance sheets. Banks experience bad debts and develop a cautious approach to lending, which continues to be seen even after the economy begins to recover. As a result, the banking sector typically lags 12–18 months behind the economic cycle.

Recovery brings with it the need for additional working capital. As economic conditions improve, so sales opportunities develop. Additional finance is needed to fund these sales opportunities, to fund additional stock, marketing expenses, new staff, etc. Bankers, however, traditionally look for audited accounts and good tangible security to support increased requests for finance. Audited accounts, however, will be historic and will reflect the weakened trading conditions seen during the recession. Asset values, especially property, will still have uncertain prices with residual equity uncertain. As a result, with improving economic conditions, businesses will have difficulty in raising additional finance from traditional banking sources. The current area of performance will be sales, whereas banks will be looking at the company's historical financial performance.

OVERTRADING OR TAKING ADVANTAGE OF BUSINESS OPPORTUNITIES?

A company seeking to take advantage of the economic cycle as it turns from recession to boom could find that it is undertaking too high a volume of business for the level of finance within the company, resulting in serious cash flow problems. Some use the parallel of a flagpole and its foundations. The higher the flagpole (i.e. sales) the deeper the level of foundations required to support it (i.e. the capital base).

Without any additional finance in the business, the expanding company will seek to squeeze out as much cash flow as possible from internal sources – trade creditors, reduced stock and tighter credit control. However, given historic recession, these areas will already have been given keen priority as part of the survival strategy. So where does the additional cash flow come from?

Bankers call it 'overtrading', whilst the entrepreneur calls it 'taking advantage of business opportunities'. The banker typically suggests consolidation, the businessperson looks at ways of financing the increasing opportunities, which have eluded them during the recession.

Factoring finance is directly linked to the current sales performance and not solely to the balance sheet, and will present a natural financing tool to satisfy the growing level of demand for working capital as the economic cycle turns from recession to boom. Economic boom itself leads to a generation of a 'sales culture', an environment ideally suited to factoring finance. Factoring will provide finance directly linked to the sales performance of a company. As the company grows so does its level of working capital funding.

BAD DEBTS

Corporate failure is a fact of business life, whatever the stage of the economic cycle. However, its incidence increases as the economy heads into recession as falling sales, rising interest rates and tighter credit take their toll on corporate survival. Equally, as the economy begins to exit recession, many companies are undercapitalised to finance the new opportunities being seen. As a result, the incidence of corporate failure tends to increase as the economy swings into and out of recession.

About 25% of the factors within the marketplace are able to offer protection against bad debts for credit approved customers. Thus the factoring market can not only provide the additional working capital needed to finance growth but also protection against bad debt loss. Factors are better placed to absorb bad debts than the clients they are protecting. Their strengthened balance sheet reserves can cope better than those who are trying to build theirs up.

FACTORS' ATTITUDES TO RISK DURING THE ECONOMIC CYCLE

Factoring companies, being commercial in their nature, react to economic activity in a similar way to most businesses. Because the factors provide finance against the area of activity of a business most influenced by general economic conditions, notably sales, they tend to be more in tune with what is happening within the economy, before the official statistics are published. In many ways the factoring industry can be seen to be the barometer of economic activity – they experience the change in economic activity some 6–9 months ahead of the formal economic statistics being published. As a result, the stage of the cycle the economy is in determines how flexible the factors will tend to be.

During recession, it is a seller's market for the financial markets as a whole, as credit becomes harder to generate. As a result the factor's attitudes to the assessment of risks change markedly. The latest experience being that of the recession of 1990–1992, the factor's assessment of risk were changing constantly. Many factors experienced losses from both their factoring and invoice discounting portfolios. As a result, there was an increased tendency towards 'flavour of the month' policies.

If a factoring company experiences a problem, be it fraud or a general bad debt loss, within a particular industry, that industry becomes very heavily scrutinised for a period with many new clients rejected due to their position within that industry. Typically, this toughened underwriting criterion lasts for a three to six month period until time puts the specific industry risk back into the history books and another industry falls under scrutiny.

As a result of several high-profile losses, invoice discounting became recognised as much higher risk, with many factors and discounters closing their doors for the provision of the service. With the factor not being directly in touch with their client's customers, problems with the invoices, i.e. their security, can not always be picked up quickly. This conservatism was further reinforced by a number of invoice discounters having controlled exits from the marketplace, selling their portfolios.

During recession, the factoring market tends towards full service factoring as a more controlled means of providing finance. Invoice discounting criteria become tougher, with general conservatism within the financial markets reinforcing the 'cherry-picking' that takes place, notwithstanding the increased enquiry level brought about by the banking sector's conservatism.

As recovery begins, however, there becomes a shift in market power towards the client. Increased confidence, associated with improving economic conditions, generates more confidence in the corporate sector generally. The factors feel more comfortable with their clients' ability to grow, and with that growth, their ability to generate increased fees. As a result, the factors' risk assessment tends to be less conservative, with the 'sales' culture taking over. Risk assessment criteria swing in the client's favour, and better

packages can be negotiated. Indeed at the time of writing, late 1994, the marketplace is beginning to become very cut-throat, with many factors competing for less risky business as they seek to build up their portfolios battered
by the recession.

Summary

The banking sector's frequent reluctance to provide further assistance to their clients
as economic conditions worsen, or as their clients expand beyond the value of their
existing resources, places the factors in the positive position of being able to support
business in every stage of the economic cycle. They view their clients' business and
financing in a commercial manner, providing support where viability is established
and their security is satisfactory.

At all stages of the economic cycle, the factoring companies adopt a commercial
attitude towards risk, still providing support in the depths of recession and in the
euphoria of a boom. Factoring and invoice discounting houses therefore present themselves as commercial financiers 'for all seasons'.

Chapter 3

The factoring market: the choice of facilities

As seen earlier, the enquiry level of the factoring industry tends to be unaffected by recession, with the factors benefiting from a cautious banking environment during recessionary times and being able to provide expansionist working capital for undercapitalised companies in time of boom. But what services are made available and do they suit every company?

The industry as a whole has a number of 'generic' facilities, which are duly segmented according to an individual client company's stage of development. As a company expands, so does its systems development. The factoring industry matches their facilities to those developmental needs.

The industry breaks down into the following areas:

1. Factoring

- recourse factoring
- non-recourse factoring
- 'commercial' recourse factoring
- merchant financing

2. Invoice discounting

- disclosed invoice discounting/agency factoring
- confidential invoice discounting
- packaged finance

3. International facilities

- export factoring
- import factoring
- export invoice discounting

1. FACTORING

Disclosed factoring represents the backbone of the services offered by the industry. Typically servicing young growing companies in their early stages of development, disclosed factoring ideally suits undercapitalised companies whose directors have few tangible personal assets to support any requirement for expansionist finance. Equally it suits companies in the early stages of their systems development, where the owner manager undertakes the multi-disciplined role of co-ordinating sales, marketing, production and finance.

Factoring provides management support services to release more of that most precious of resources – time – time to concentrate on more productive and profitable activities. Instead of undertaking the credit control function and deviating from their core activities, this can be out sourced to a professional third party. This also allows the role of salesperson and credit controller to be separated, allowing the factor to undertake the 'bad guy' role, thereby not conflicting with the positive sales side of the business.

How does factoring work?

In its essence, factoring is very simple (Figure 3.1). The client raises their invoices in the normal way, forwarding one to their customer and a copy to the factor. On the invoice will be an 'assignment' stamp which details that the debt has been assigned to the client's factor, whom alone can receive payment to discharge the debt.

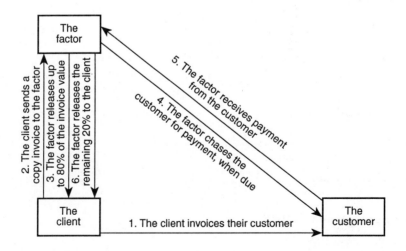

Figure 3.1   How factoring works

The factor will then release the agreed percentage of the invoice value, up to 85%, with the customer then chased for payment, when due. The unfinanced portion of the invoice is returned to the client upon receipt of payment from the customer. The client is charged an administration fee for the credit control and a discount rate, the equivalent of bank interest for the funds drawn down from the factor.

Two types of factoring exist:

- recourse factoring
- non-recourse factoring (sometimes called full service factoring).

Both facilities provide the client with the financial facility, together with credit control, credit information, and sales ledger administration. Non-recourse factoring, however, provides the added benefit of protection against bad debts.

Recourse factoring case study

Seevent Plastics Ltd manufactures and prints polythene bags. Established in July 1987 from an asset purchase of a rundown business, the company was caught in an all too familiar position – a bulging order book but insufficient cash flow to finance it.

Offering a wide product range, including heavy coal sacks, thin sheets used to wrap sausages and a wide range of applications in between, their customers included British Rail and IBM among its many customers. Order books were so full that a substantial investment was needed to meet the ever-growing demand. The banks were unwilling to back the company beyond its existing levels, with a cash-flow gap created by the surge in demand for its products. Ken Fisher, director, approached Alex Lawrie.

Since Seevent Plastics has been with Alex Lawrie turnover is up almost 40% on the previous year to just under £1 million, and continues to expand. Until Seevent took on the services of a factor, Ken and his wife, the only fulltime office staff, had to face the time-consuming job of chasing up payment. With the factor relieving them of this task they have had more time to concentrate on running the company itself. Ken summarises:

> The factor's charge for this service is no more costly than employing our own credit controller and so it has already paid for itself, as well as helping get our invoices settled more quickly.

And his view of the facility?

> It has certainly been a major factor in our success.

Source: adapted from an Alex Lawrie case study.

Non-recourse factoring

In addition to their core services, a number of factors offer protection against bad debts. Whilst providing peace of mind to a client company, non-recourse factoring also provides a valuable in-depth source of credit information regarding clients' customers.

Non-recourse factoring case study

Glenmere Timber, one of the most successful sawmilling companies in the UK, have been with Close Invoice Finance for 10 years. From humble origins their headquarters now stretch over nine acres, with new offices, substantial investment in state-of-the-art drying kilns and 200 000 square ft of under-cover storage. Glenmere are now one of the UK's largest stockists of North American hardwoods.

It is still however, very much a family-managed business, with no fewer than seven family members having various executive responsibilities. Glenmere's main customers are the furniture industry, joinery and refurbishment trades, and annual sales have grown substantially over the years.

Keen to ensure that there is no danger of the business returning to its humble origins, Mr R. Robinson, Managing Director, makes full use of the expertise and advice available to him as part of his non-recourse factoring arrangement with Close Invoice Finance. Close provide Glenmere with an 80% prepayment against outstanding invoices, a complete sales ledger and credit control service, and a funding facility that grows in line with their sales.

Glenmere are covered by 100% bad debt protection on all approved invoices and can obtain an up-to-date credit profile of any company with whom they are considering doing business with. Mr Robinson encourages his sales people to contact Close before making a sale, let alone taking on business. Credit experts at Close provide them with substantial credit information and track record data on the customer, giving the sales person a clear picture of their prospective customer. The decision whether to go ahead always rests with Glenmere.

With such market intelligence at their fingertips, Glenmere have no need to worry about bad debts, giving them the freedom to concentrate on what they are best at – building the business.

Mr Robinson is a great advocate of factoring, stating: 'You get paid because you use factoring'.

Source: Close Invoice Finance Ltd

'Commercial' recourse factoring

The independent factoring sector has emerged as a highly competitive alternative to the 'mainstream' sector, although representing a very small percentage of the marketplace. When a company is introduced to a commercial recourse factor, having experienced the mainstream marketplace, they seldom look back.

The services offered by the commercial recourse factors (CRFs), whilst broadly similar in their delivery to standard recourse factoring, are typically more commercial in their nature. This is born out of the need to offer a competitive alternative to their mainstream competitors. In most cases, the CRFs are smaller independent organisations, where lines of communication are short, decisions are quick, and the treatment of a client is more commercial.

The focus of attention for the CRF is on the spread and age of the customer base. Providing the client's spread of customers is good (i.e. the major customer typically comprises less than 20–25% of the outstanding sales ledger), the goods are clear of dispute and the outstanding debts are collected in less than 90 days past due date, the commercial recourse factor will generally finance all sales.

CRFs do not set credit limits on a client's customers. Instead, they recognise the close relationship held between a client and their customer, and allow the client free reign to deal with whom they wish, subject to the major customer not exceeding the established spread threshold. The CRF in many cases also allows the client to become actively involved in the chasing of their customers, working alongside their client to achieve the same goal – collecting in monies quickly whilst maintaining good relations.

Commercial recourse factoring case study

Classique Components Ltd has been successfully trading since setting up in 1992. They specialize in supplying quality hardware components to the window industry, and using their hands-on expertise from within a national company have succeeded in driving the company forward, culminating in a current turnover of c £1m per annum. Their recent experience of changing to a commercial recourse factor reflects the additional benefits that such a facility can bring.

Originally they were factoring with a bank-owned factoring company, who provided them with a standard recourse factoring facility. As part of the day to day operations of the facility, the factor assessed each of the client's customers from a credit point of view, and set finance limits in line with those assessments. The result was an ever changing cashflow, changing according to the limits set by the factor. Equally, only £15k of their major customer (£39k) was being financed, restricting the client's cashflow.

They approached a commercial recourse factor, County Factors Ltd, who do not generally set credit limits on their clients' customers. County took a view of the spread of the client's customer base, and agreed to fund the client's major customer in full, provided it did not exceed 30% of the sales ledger and providing there was no adverse credit information related to that customer. With a combination of other customers not needing to be credit assessed by the factor, the client generated an additional 20% funding from their new factoring facility, allowing a more positive approach to be adopted in financing new business opportunities.

Merchant financing – factoring without affecting the balance sheet

Merchant financing is a relatively new form of 'quasi-factoring', which until very recently has been the domain of a number of 'niche' financiers. It has its roots within factoring, but has legal and logistical differences (Figure 3.2) which give it extra flexibility compared to a standard factoring facility.

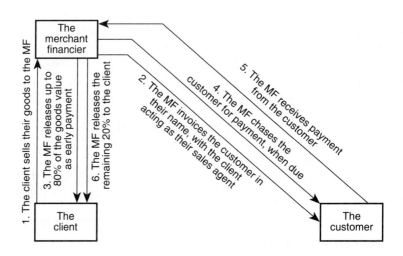

Figure 3.2   How merchant financing works

A merchant financier does not take assignment to the book debts as a factor does. Instead, the goods are actually purchased by them, taking full title to the goods. The merchant financier then sells the goods to the client's customer with the client acting as their sales agent. In this way, the merchant financier becomes a customer, and therefore a debtor of the client, not its factor.

Once the merchant financier has received confirmation that the goods have been received and accepted as satisfactory by the customer and in accordance with their purchase order, an 'early payment' is made to the client for the purchase of the products, generally up to 80% of the invoice value, with the MF taking a discount, i.e. their fees. The customer then pays the merchant financier for the goods when due, with the remaining 20% of the invoice duly returned to the client, less any further discount charges incurred.

Because the merchant financier takes title to the goods, the responsibility for the debt between the financier and the customer lies with the financier. To this end, the merchant financier will only finance the transaction providing:

- The end customer can be underwritten by the credit insurance marketplace.
- Signed acceptance of the goods purchased is received from the customer.

In this way, the merchant financier's 'downside' risks are covered. If the client's customer ceased to trade, the debt is credit insured. The customer technically has no right to dispute the outstanding debt to the financier having signed their acceptance of the goods received. As a result, the merchant financier can finance individual transactions or single customers, situations a standard factor would never contemplate undertaking.

Whilst similar in its modus operandi to factoring, it can be considered to be truly 'off-balance' sheet finance. The financier will become a debtor on the client's balance sheet, but only for the unfinanced proportion of the debt.

Because the transaction is merely a purchase and resell of goods and not an assignment of debt, as in a factoring arrangement, the facility does not directly affect a banker's security. Unlike a factor, which undertakes assignment of the book debts, the merchant financier becomes a debtor in the client's balance sheet – a debtor which makes an early payment to the client.

Readers should be aware, however, that a bank covenant regarding the debtor cover for the overdraft (i.e. debtor book/overdraft facility) may be affected by the direct reduction in the debtor book size by receiving early payment from the merchant financier. Equally, some MFs may seek to take a debenture over the business. Although this security will rank behind the principal lender, the bank will potentially be aware of the MF's involvement, and may seek to alter their existing lending.

Whilst it is always advisable for a client to inform their bankers of the arrangement, one of the key selling points often laboured by the merchant financiers is that the bank overdraft will technically remain unaffected.

Merchant finance case study

A company exporting security products to the USA and turning over approximately £2m per annum required an additional £50k of working capital to fund increased orders from their US customer. Their bankers, although having supported them for the 14 years they had been in business and allowed a gearing ratio of 200%, felt unable to support the client company's immediate cash flow requirement without the benefit of additional personal security.

The bank had a covenant of two times debtor and stock cover for the overdraft facility, and calculations showed that a full factoring or invoice discounting facility would not provide any net benefit to the company in terms of additional cash flow. So to fund the increased orders being generated from the USA a facility was set up with a merchant financier.

Having established the satisfactory creditworthiness of the company's customer, the merchant financier was able to provide funding up to $100k against the customer's account. Whilst markedly more expensive than a factoring service, the flexibility of being able to offer the one sales ledger account to the merchant financier to fund their additional cash flow requirement on an 'as needs' basis was enjoyed. The bank overdraft facilities were unaffected and the additional working capital they needed was generated.

One of the merchant financiers, Fairfax Gerrad Ltd, have extended the merchant financing concept to include services. A client of theirs had a good quality customer account which was due to pay a regular quarterly royalty payment of £100k. Their existing bank facilities were limited and fully utilised. The deal was structured by means of a bill of exchange made payable to the merchant financier who then offered early payment to the client company.

Again the bank facilities were unaffected but the client had the benefit of additional cash flow.

2. INVOICE DISCOUNTING

As companies grow, so their internal systems develop more effectively. As these systems develop, so the need for third party involvement is minimised. Equally, with cheap access to information technology and associated accounting packages, the need for sales ledger administration is removed. All in all, growing companies that are turning over in excess of £1m per annum can typically outgrow the tangible benefits a full factoring facility can offer. Access to growing finance can however, provide the cash-flow solution required to fulfilling their growth plans. The factor, however, requires control over their security in order to consider advancing funds. And so we have a conundrum. The client has the systems and resources to run their own sales ledger and credit control. The factor, on the other hand wants to ensure they have control.

Two products have evolved within the market which offer the financial benefits of factoring but allow the client company to maintain full control of the sales ledger administration – agency factoring and invoice discounting.

Agency factoring (sometimes called bulk factoring)

To a company, agency factoring presents a natural progression from factoring. Where the company has performed profitably and has developed the necessary systems to chase its own debts effectively, agency factoring provides finance that grows whilst allowing the client company to chase its own debts. In this way the company has the benefit of expanding working capital whilst controlling the credit control function.

Under an agency agreement (Figure 3.3) the client acts as the factor's **agent** in collecting the debts. The debts are **assigned** to the factoring company in a similar way to a factoring client via the **assignment stamp** on the client's invoices. The customer, whilst chased by the client company, discharges the debt by paying the factor directly.

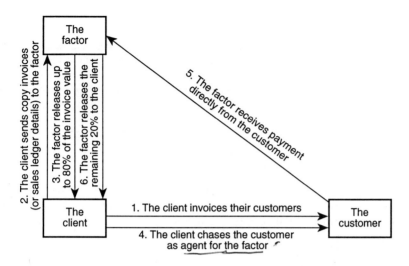

Figure 3.3 How agency factoring works

Typically, this facility represents a half-way house between factoring and invoice discounting, which allows the client to maintain full contact with their customers whilst giving the factor some control. The customers are aware of the factor's involvement, and are required to pay the factor directly.

Under an agency agreement, the factor will run a parallel sales ledger, with the result that the cost of the facility will mostly be more expensive than its invoice discounting counterpart.

Agency case study

A computer hardware distributor had been in business for around three years, progressing to around £1.2m turnover. During this time they had traded using a £30k bank overdraft facility. Although profitable and having a net worth of about £60k, the levels of net profit generated were insufficient to meet the company's cash-flow needs. The company sought to use their creditors as their means of financing growth while, at the same time, they were collecting their debts in approximately 45–50 days, operating a very tight credit control regime.

Owing to the use of creditors to finance the business, the company had stretched their creditors to the point where they had 21 County Court Judgements (CCJs) against them, endemic of severe 'overtrading'.

Whilst concerned at the level of CCJs against the company, the discounter took the commercial view of them as a sign of positive growth rather than a company about to fail. When combined with the company's creditable credit management performance, and recognising that the company only needed a limited level of finance, approximately 65% against the debtors, an agency facility was made available. The financial performance alone would have just qualified them for an invoice discounting facility, although the discounter wanted an element of control through customer disclosure, in view of the historic CCJs.

Confidential invoice discounting

Confidential invoice discounting represents the flagship facility for the industry and the ideal facility for most companies. Under the confidential invoice discounting (CID) facility the factor's involvement is limited, with the disclosure to the customer removed totally (Figure 3.4).

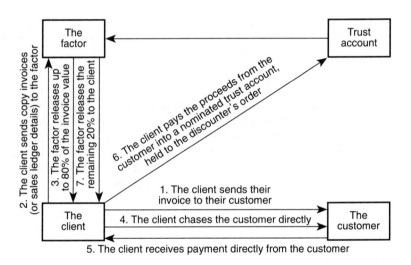

Figure 3.4   How invoice discounting works

Instead of controlling the risks by disclosure to the customer and insisting upon payment being received directly, the factor allows the client full control over their sales ledger, enabling the client/customer relationship to be maintained in full. The client receives payments directly from their customers. These payments are paid into a trust account held to the discounter's order. To support their risk management, the discounter carries out regular audits, either monthly or quarterly, on the client's sales ledger to validate its security.

The discounter's principal concern is that of fraudulent activity by their clients. With no disclosure or direct contact with the client's customers fraudulent invoices may be submitted of which the discounter will be unaware. However, fraudulent activity usually stems from financial instability, whereby the client has a higher need for cash flow than their sources of finance can provide.

For invoice discounting to be sanctioned, the discounter must feel satisfied that no pressure will be brought to bear upon their client's own cash flow to make them undertaking fraudulent activity, e.g. submit false invoicing details. Although monthly reporting requirements by the factor should highlight certain disturbing trends, which can trigger quick remedial action, it could be the quarterly audit before misinformation is picked up. To qualify for confidential invoice discounting, therefore, a client must have good control systems and must demonstrate clear financial success. The facility in certain circumstances may be operated by certain discounters with disclosure made to the client's customers, although the facility operates in the same way as a confidential facility.

Invoice discounting case study

Winning a prestigious Business Award in 1994; turning losses into profit; earning a reputation for being innovative, ambitious and capable of producing results would be enough for most businessmen, but not for Leon Shepperdson, Chairman and Managing Director of STAMCO. His goal is to lead a best practice company in every sphere of its operation and to provide twice the number of jobs for his home town, within the next five years. Quite a tall order for any business but for a man whose aphorism is 'work is fun', he has already proved that anything is achievable.

Founded in 1957, STAMCO are timber merchants. With a workforce of 85 employees, in 1994 the company achieved a turnover of £5.9m and profits of £104 000, an increase of 102% on the previous year. Since 1991 STAMCO have experienced a period of massive change, particularly in the culture of the business. A cycle of examination, measurement, invention and change has been directed towards producing timber which is the right quality, at the right price and available right away for a growing customer base. 'We achieve these goals by focusing on training, customer care and a willingness to implement improvements to bottom-line results', explains Mr Shepperdson. 'The backbone to this process is a strong cashflow and good credit management.'

To maintain this robust cashflow STAMCO have used, since June 1992, a confidential invoice discounting facility from Griffin Factors. 'It makes sense to us to have in place a finance facility that most closely meets our on-going cashflow requirements,' says Mr Shepperdson. With invoice discounting cash keeps pace with sales. Griffin provides up to 80% of the value of invoices immediately they are raised, the remainder when STAMCO's customers pay. 'Although invoice discounting is a confidential service my philosophy is if something works, and works well, why not shout about it?' says Mr Shepperdson.

In addition to the finance, Griffin also provide credit protection against customer insolvency. 'At STAMCO we have never subscribed to a doom and gloom outlook. With protection against bad debts we have been able to shelter our-selves from some of the worst effects of the recent recession. Throughout we have been able to concentrate on improving delivery times, providing what our customers want and creating a business that people want to work for.'

'STAMCO's ambition has always been to make a difference to customers, sup-pliers and staff. Looking at our recent achievements I can confidently claim we have made an impact. Building on this, next year we aim to break the £7 mil-lion turnover barrier and achieve profits of £300k – both targets look achiev-able.' concludes Mr Shepperdson.

Packaged finance

In recent years, some product development has been introduced within the marketplace – that of packaged finance. Under packaged finance, additional security is taken by the discounter, to provide an element of 'top-up' facility. By examining the cash flows of a given profitable client, the level of working capital requirement can be gauged in relation to the security available. Using invoice discounting as the core source of security, other assets can be used to provide additional security to support short-term requirements over the top of the usage from invoice discounting, e.g. stock (Figure 3.5).

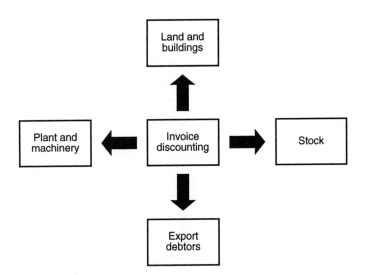

Figure 3.5 Packaged finance

Whilst the idea of advancing finance against other assets besides the debtor book is not innovative in its own right, the marketing of the product under the 'packaged finance' banner was the first marketing inroad into offering serious competition to traditional bank finance. The packaged finance service can enable the client to have access to an expanding facility, which can mirror their direct cash-flow requirements.

In its simplest format, packaged finance operates an element of stock finance. Finance is made available from the existing stocking levels, subject to the stock being able to be valued effectively. The total level of finance offered to the client including the top-up facility, however, will typically not exceed 95–100% of the total debtor book.

International trade finance facilities can also be raised in a similar way. Goods can be brought into the country via a revolving letter of credit facility using the debtor book as security for the letter of credit. Once the goods are shipped to the customers, so invoices are created which enable finance to be released to repay the letter of credit raised.

Additionally, other financial facilities such as duty deferment bonds and supplier bonds (where the packaged financier agrees to pay a supplier directly from the proceeds of invoices submitted) can be raised in this way, using invoice discounting as the core product against which the finance is securitised.

The 'packaged finance' concept is slowly beginning to spread into the factoring marketplace.

Packaged finance case study

Established in 1985, Data Peripherals provides a comprehensive service in mass data storage. The managing director, Peter Brophy, attributes the company's achievements and growth to the high standards he wanted to set as the hallmark of his business together with the financial and business support provided by his factoring company.

In addition to a traditional factoring facility, his factor, Venture Factors PLC, provided the company with a stock facility, i.e. a line of credit made available against their levels of stock. In addition to the standard benefits attributed to a traditional factoring facility, Mr Brophy added:

> ...[the factor's] willingness to provide stock finance gave the company the crucial resource we needed to get to the critical point from which to grow. Since then we have been able to attract new equity and funding from shareholders but it is a comfort to know that, in case of need, I can turn to Venture.

3. INTERNATIONAL FACILITIES

With the increased propensity to develop new markets, export facilities offered by the factoring market, though small in terms of the relative size of the marketplace, are steadily beginning to increase in importance. Much of the key information relating to international facilities is highlighted within dedicated chapters on both facilities, and it is not proposed to double count on later chapters, with the exception of detailing its mechanics (Figure 3.6).

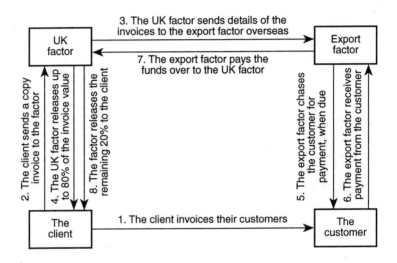

Figure 3.6   How two-factor export factoring works

In the UK export factoring is undertaken by most of the ABF&D members, as an additional facility for those clients in the international sphere. Whilst most factors use corresponding factors in the respective overseas countries to chase and underwrite the debts in the respective overseas countries, some have sought to directly chase overseas debts using linguistic skills based in the UK. Whilst this doesn't offer the same local presence, it can offer a marked cost saving through to clients, although the service is unlikely to be as effective.

Technology and service provision

As computer technology has developed, so the factors and discounters have sought to improve their service quality, whilst at the same time generating substantial cost savings for both the client and themselves. To this end, computer links have been developed by most of the larger factors, which enable the client to have access, via a password system, to the factor's computer system.

The computer link enables the client to have up-to-date access to information which enables them to make more effective decisions with regard to the financing and credit management of their respective businesses. It enables queries to be examined at hours to suit the client company, offering increased flexibility to the client's needs.

Developments have been extended to include direct input of invoices into the factor's computer, enabling a theoretical turnaround of 24 hours between raising invoices and receiving cash into the bank.

Driven by the desire to generate productivity improvements and reductions in their cost base, together with keeping their clients informed and satisfied, many of the factors have used information technology to its fullest improvements in the quality of service provided.

New product development

The factoring marketplace is competitive, with some 62 providers of finance. The factors have historically shown themselves to be fast moving in terms of reacting to changing market conditions, and quickly realigning their assessment criteria. As a result, one would naturally expect new products to be launched on a regular basis. Not so – new product development has been very slow to progress through the marketplace.

Naturally, during recessionary periods, new product development takes a back seat as factors seek to concentrate on their existing activities, as recession begins to hit them and their clients. Risk becomes the centre of attention rather than that of client service, with new product development a secondary issue.

Instrumental in the lack of product development is the healthy underlying growth being experienced within the marketplace. With the marketplace having grown on an annual basis by around 20% since 1983, a conservative culture has been generated within the industry as a whole. After all, if the senior management within the industry are targeted by their parent financial institution for a given return on capital, why commit heavy resources to developing new products, when profit levels have been typically consistent from standard, core products?

If the marketplace were mature, however, undoubtedly the factors would be competing very heavily against each other for their business, with 'musical clients' being prevalent. Their very survival would lead to developments into new areas previously untouched, e.g. the construction industry. With its contractual nature, tight terms and conditions and its natural propensity for dispute, this market sector and others of a similar type remain totally untapped. They do not present a straightforward means of providing finance securely to the factors. If market pressure were brought to bear, undoubtedly solutions would be forthcoming – after all, 'necessity becomes the mother of invention'.

Technology also places severe restrictions upon new product development. By the very nature of the industry, most factors are slaves to their own computer systems. The services provided involve the use of complex computer networks and the use of bespoke software developed by in-house development teams over many years. As a result, the 'central nervous system' creates an environment of fixed ideas, restricting the potential flexibility to clients and the development of new products – many of the factors are systems-led rather than client-led. Whilst new fourth and fifth generation developmental tools will undoubtedly ease the production of new programmes and changes to the existing systems, the systems themselves are so complex and intertwined as to make radical changes very difficult. Equally, 'technophobia' is prevalent within most operational staff within the factoring companies, restricting the practical implementation of new ideas through the use of personal computers.

Another key reason for conservatism within new product development is the very structural nature of the industry. The industry's core product is cash, with substantial funds required to run a portfolio. As a result, the majority of factoring companies are backed by financial institutions, who maintain control of their funds by retaining all of the equity. Thus, rather than being run by entrepreneurs, who would have a stake in the equity of the business, standing to improve or lose their investment according to their performance, factoring companies are run by professional managers, whose entrepreneurial flair is influenced directly by the parent bank's attitude to their subsidiary.

This is particularly highlighted within the ABF&D marketplace. Only two of the smaller independent factors (who between them control around 6% of the marketplace) have released any equity through to the management – and even then it is only 2.5% and 5% respectively.

Whilst some of the mainstream factors' management teams may have parent bank shares as options, the number offered are immaterial by comparison to their parent bank's capitalisation. Equally, the factoring divisions return such a small profit contribution to the parent bank's overall profit levels that their collective performance is hardly going to affect the share price of the parent banks. As a by-product of being professional managers, there is always someone looking over their shoulders – there is no freedom to fail, little freedom to experiment.

Finally, the risks of getting a new product wrong create a conservative culture. New product development can present a high-risk strategy to a conservatively placed market sector. A factor can potentially lose their whole investment in a client if they get the new product wrong.

With perhaps the exception of the 'packaged finance' product originally launched by TSB Samuel Commercial Finance Ltd (originally Hill Samuel Commercial Finance) and some developments in the 'niche' merchant finance sector, very few new products have been seen in the marketplace in recent years. Some attempts have been seen historically to diversify, e.g. stock confirmation facilities being added to the core factoring services available, although these have been very short lived, with the respective factors reverting to their core products.

Experience from the USA

The USA continues to stand out as the world leader in the factoring industry. With its established history, and its natural propensity to new product development, the trends within this market can generate a good idea of how the market may develop over the coming years. In the USA, commercial finance organisations have taken over from where the factors have left off.

The US disclosed factoring market is very developed having emanated from and remaining primarily within the textile sector. This market sector has felt comfortable with disclosure to the client's customer base. However, in the early part of the 20th century, the first commercial finance organisation was set up, providing sales-linked finance without disclosure being required to the client's customers, and being provided on a 'recourse' basis, i.e. in the event of the client's customers defaulting on payment, the debt would be reassigned to the client, with no protection offered against bad debts.

Commercial finance began in earnest in the early 1950s. It has now become an industry advancing in excess of $100bn of funding lent at the end of 1993. Factoring companies, whose statistics are based upon their client turnover comprising some $57bn of client turnover at the end of 1993. With approximately $6bn of funding provided (on the assumption of 10% of client turnover being taken as funding, an approximate rule of thumb) the factoring market funds the equivalent of 6% of the commercial finance market.

The commercial finance market is well entrenched within the US marketplace, offering other finance packages in addition to receivables financing. To this end, they can consider inventory financing as well as other assets. As Sidney Rutberg commented in a recent article about the trends within the US commercial finance market:[1]

> The future looks bright for the commercial finance industry. [US] Banking is becoming more of a money management and investment banking business than a commercial lending enterprise. More and more, banks are de-emphasising the pedestrian business of making loans in favour of more sophisticated, if perhaps riskier, enterprises. The big profits for major banks are coming from currency trading, securities underwriting and dealing in derivatives.

This has left the lending business wide open for asset-based lenders who are and who will continue to fill in the gaps as banks seek more adventurous activities.

Leonard Machlis, the executive director of the Commercial Finance Association, which has been in existence for over 50 years, summed up the culture of the stateside marketplace:

> The US Commercial finance marketplace is highly entrepreneurial. As soon as a vacuum develops it is quickly filled. Institutions are prepared to look at new areas of operation.

He quotes that in the USA the market is developing to include niche players who will finance single invoices, and indeed institutions who will fund receivables within the construction sector.

And of the future for the commercial finance marketplace?

> ...in time all corporate lending will be on a commercial financing basis.

The future of new product development in the UK marketplace

Given the size of the marketplace and the size of the companies within it, one would expect more flexibility and entrepreneurial spirit than currently exists. Whilst the marketplace has some good quality individuals within it, many of the senior managers of the industry have grown up within a factoring culture alone, and have fixed ideas about running a factoring company. As a result, there is a natural resistance to develop away from the core products.

In our view, as the market begins to develop further, new product development will be critical to success, with the UK market following the States' example. With the factors and discounters being so close to their clients' financial performance, they should be able to provide the additional flexibility to their clients by financing other assets within their clients' business.

Undoubtedly, the new product development will emanate from those factors and discounters which are independent of the high street banks. Not having the branch network to rely upon as 'warm' introducers of business, and not having to cope with the wider issue of 'competing' with their parent banks, the independent players will need to provide services of better quality, which offer added value to their clients in order to compete against their mainstream counterparts who will have the benefits of greater economies of scale.

Indeed, as the market continues to expand so there will be a filtration of new ideas as finance professionals transfer their skills across the financial services sector. New product development will evolve, but will evolve slowly with the inherent structure of the industry restricting the brave decisions that need to be taken.

Summary

The factoring market offers a choice of facility, facilities which successfully cater for individual companies' stage of development, with their respective balance sheets and credit management skills determining which facility is made available. The underlying market structure, however, typically generates a risk-averse culture, with new product development seen to be slow.

The market, however, is showing early signs of moving towards the American model of commercial finance, with some organisations now starting to provide finance against other assets such as stock. Whilst this trend has taken a relatively low profile to date, we should expect it to develop further as the factors begin to face an increasingly competitive marketplace and strive for competitive advantage.

NOTES

1 'The secured lender', published by the Commercial Finance Association, New York, June 1994, p.46.

Chapter 4

The factor's perspective: how factors assess the client

If the client goes bust, can we collect out?

These words echo at most credit committee hearings when assessing the risks within a new business proposal. Can the advanced funds be fully realised from the outstanding invoices in a terminal situation?

As we have mentioned before, whilst an important consideration in their risk assessment, factors do not just consider themselves as 'pawnbrokers', looking solely at their security. It is this latter view which has stigmatised the factoring industry since the early 1970s, with many business and financial people historically labelling the industry as 'finance of last resort finance', the last ditch attempt to save a company from the abyss of insolvency.

Factoring companies are keen to establish relationships which provide them with long-term income flows and their clients with the means to fulfil their sales ambitions, with commercialism echoing this philosophy:

- The upfront expense of generating new business means that it can be around 12 months before a client begins to generate an actual profit for the factoring company.
- The costs of realising security upon a client's insolvency involves the extensive use of resources and associated expense, potentially removing any historic profit generated. Equally the factor is exposed to potential bad debt loss.
- The dangers of the factor being exposed to fraudulent activity increase directly when a company is experiencing financial difficulty.

As a result, the quality of the factor's security, whilst essential in assessing a given proposal, does not represent the sole criterion for support.

ASSESSING THE PROPOSAL

In assessing a given proposal, three areas of risk are primarily considered:

1. financial performance of the client company;
2. quality of the security;
3. quality of management.

1. Financial performance

The factor's security will only be tested if the company being financed ceases to trade. It is at this time that the lending decisions made by the factor will be proved. As a result, the financial position of the potential client is an important issue in assessing the likely length of relationship the factor will enjoy with a client, and the risk of needing to recoup their funds.

The importance of the company's financial performance depends upon the facility being sought. Typically, the weighting of financial performance to security in the risk assessment varies according to the factor's perceived risk of the facilities offered (Table 4.1).

Table 4.1 Comparison of weightings of financial performance to security

Factoring	Financial performance	25%
	Security	75%
Disclosed invoice discounting	Financial performance	35%
	Security	65%
Confidential invoice discounting	Financial performance	50%
	Security	50%

In assessing the financial performance of a given company, financial ratios are analysed from both audited and management figures. These are examined not only for their own performance but also on a trend basis, which highlights why factors usually require three years of audited accounts before offering facilities.

Ratios are analysed within the following principal areas:

- stability
- profitability
- liquidity.

Stability

The level of shareholder's commitment to the business is crucial – after all what have the shareholders got to lose if the business fails? Equally, how motivated are the management to secure their investment? To this end, the level of gearing is closely examined.

gearing = total external borrowings/tangible net worth[1]

As has been seen only too often within postwar recessions, highly-geared companies are the most vulnerable to adverse fluctuations in interest rates, with insolvency an all too common route when the serviceability of the borrowings is compromised by a downturn in income generation.

Typically, under a factoring facility, gearing is not regarded critically. For invoice discounting, however, it is regarded more rigorously. A number of factors and discounting houses will restrict the levels of finance advanced to a multiple of the tangible net worth of a business, usually a ratio of 5–7 times net worth for disclosed invoice discounting and 2.5–3.5 times net worth for confidential invoice discounting.

Profitability

Factors ideally want to support expanding profitable companies, and will examine two key profitability ratios:

gross margin = gross profit/net sales
pre-tax net margin = pre-tax net profit/net sales

The gross margins will be considered against the performance of the client's industry, whilst the net profit figure will generally be looked at in regards the client's overall performance. The profits generated and those within a client's forward projections will be critically analysed to take into consideration the client's ability to meet the additional costs associated with the factoring facility itself.

Liquidity

This is perhaps the most important area of financial consideration for the factor – how effective is a client's cash flow? Owing to the factor providing short-term working capital, the ability to pay liabilities as and when they fall due presents the key information in determining the underlying cash flow of the business. The liquidity ratios typically examined by the factor are:

current ratio = current assets/current liabilities [1]

An ideal current ratio of 200% is considered satisfactory within the traditional credit management manuals, although a current ratio in excess of 100% is generally acceptable within the factoring industry.

acid test = (current assets – stocks)/current liabilities [2]

This determines how quickly near cash assets can be turned into cash. It gives a very clear indication of the underlying cash flow of the business, and 80–100% is considered satisfactory.

debt turn = trade debtors × 365/sales [3]

Perhaps the most important liquidity ratio for a factor. This shows the number of days' sales outstanding, and is indicative of the client's ability to collect their debts. The factor will closely scrutinise a client's debt turn performance, as they have a much closer idea than most financial institutions of what is expected from a given industry and will judge a given client's performance accordingly.[2]

$$\text{credit turn} = \text{trade creditors} \times 365/\text{purchases} \qquad [4]$$

The credit turn reflects any likely creditor pressure that may exist. The higher the credit turn, the more the client company is delaying payment to its suppliers, the more likely cash flow pressures are going to exist.

$$\text{stock turn} = \text{purchases/closing stock} \qquad [5]$$

The slower the turning of stocks, the more the level of working capital tied up. Overstocking is a key determinant of tight cash flow and the associated need for cash. It can equally indicate that substantial dead stock may be held, which will have little value thus reducing the 'real' net worth of the business

The use of ratio analysis

Any audited accounts produced by external parties will reflect the at best position for a company. Whilst not seeking to cook the books, some year end activity can suggest they may have been 'slightly roasted'. As a result, the standard ratio analysis will provide the at best analysis of a company's financial position.

However, in using ratio analysis, automatic answers are not provided for the factor, rather they will produce a list of further questions in assessing the proposal:

How have the ratios changed over time and what have been the commercial influences within the client's business and industry underlying these changes?

If the liquidity ratios have changed are there clear reasons as to why the changes have been seen? If the changes have been negative, could these cast a question mark over the viability of the business as a whole.

For example, if stock turnover has slowed is it indicative of slow moving stock that may need to be written off, or a strategic change to higher margin, slower moving stock? If the debt turn has worsened, has the quality of the customer base worsened over the year such that they are paying slower, are there extensive bad debts or is it just indicative of a lack of management control?

By judging the ratios in tandem with various face to face meetings held with their clients, the factor can get a feel for the client and their viability.

How do the ratios compare to standard industry norms?

Each industry will have its own typical profile, which makes it difficult to directly compare industry by industry. It would, for example be wrong to compare ratios between say a haulage company and other industries.

Hauliers will tend to be highly geared, through the necessity to finance the vehicles used to undertake their activity, whilst at the same time being illiquid (i.e. the current ratio being below 100%) through high capital repayments, reflected within current liabilities.

Other industries will have completely different profiles owing to the different capital structure of the businesses.

Figure 4.1 shows the internal appraisal spreadsheet of Venture Factors plc, which details the key ratios examined in their internal assessments of client companies.

Intangible features

The factor will not just look at the ratios in considering the financial position of the client company. Other 'intangible' features influence their assessment:

The quality of the client's auditors

A factor is more likely to look favourably upon a client whose auditors are well known and known to be of quality, e.g. one of the top six. In general, the greater the funds required, the more reliance is placed upon this feature.

Qualifications within the accounts

The accounts may be qualified by the client company's auditors, who do not feel comfortable with specific areas of the company's operation. If the client company's auditors cannot express an opinion on the validity of the accounts, what value will they have for a financier? A qualification on the valuing of a company's stocks will cast doubts upon the stock figures contained within the accounts. As a result, gross profitability could be overstated, and the net worth affected.

A number of accounts are produced on a 'going concern basis', i.e. relying upon external financiers to allow the continuance of trade. In all cases of 'qualifications', without further direct information from the auditors, the factor may seek to decline a given proposal.

Propensity for fraud

One of the key reasons behind closely assessing the financial performance of a given business is that the weaker the company, the greater the need for finance and the greater the propensity to defraud. If cash flow is weak, and the business is facing insolvency, a dichotomy is presented to the shareholders – do they let the business fail and lose everything they have built up,

```
                                        VENTURE FACTORS PLC.

Client Name    :
Auditors       :
-----------------------------------|------------------|------------------|------------------|
Period End                         |                  |                  |                  |
Months in Period                   |     Months       |     Months       |     Months       |
Aud/QSF/Qual/Man                   |                  |                  |                  |
-----------------------------------|------------------|------------------|------------------|
Turnover                           |  0.0   ERROR     |  0.0   ERROR     |  0.0   ERROR     |
Gross Profit                       |  0.0   ERROR     |  0.0   ERROR     |  0.0   ERROR     |
Pre Tax Net Profit (Loss)          |  0.0   ERROR     |  0.0   ERROR     |  0.0   ERROR     |
after: Interest Paid               |  0.0             |  0.0             |  0.0             |
       Directors Remun/Drawing     |  0.0             |  0.0             |  0.0             |
       Depreciation                |  0.0             |  0.0             |  0.0             |
Dividends                          |         0.0      |         0.0      |         0.0      |
Taxation                           |         0.0      |         0.0      |         0.0      |
....                               |         0.0      |         0.0      |         0.0      |
Retained Profit/(loss)             |         0.0      |         0.0      |         0.0      |
Opening Tangible Net Worth         |         0.0      |         0.0      |         0.0      |
New Capital                        |         0.0      |         0.0      |         0.0      |
Goodwill                           |         0.0      |         0.0      |         0.0      |
Closing Tangible Net Worth         |         0.0      |         0.0      |         0.0      |
-----------------------------------|------------------|------------------|------------------|
FIXED ASSETS                       |                  |                  |                  |
Land & Buildings                   |  0.0             |  0.0             |  0.0             |
Plant & Machinery                  |  0.0             |  0.0             |  0.0             |
Vehicles                           |  0.0             |  0.0             |  0.0             |
Other                              |  0.0             |  0.0             |  0.0             |
....                               |  0.0   0.0       |  0.0   0.0       |  0.0   0.0       |
                                   |------------------|------------------|------------------|
                                   |         0.0      |         0.0      |         0.0      |
                                   |------------------|------------------|------------------|
INVESTMENTS                        |                  |                  |                  |
Subsidiary Company                 |  0.0             |  0.0             |  0.0             |
Other                              |  0.0   0.0       |  0.0   0.0       |  0.0   0.0       |
                                   |------------------|------------------|------------------|
                                   |         0.0      |         0.0      |         0.0      |
                                   |------------------|------------------|------------------|
CURRENT ASSETS                     |                  |                  |                  |
Cash                               |  0.0             |  0.0             |  0.0             |
Trade Debtors                      |  0.0             |  0.0             |  0.0             |
Other Debtors                      |  0.0             |  0.0             |  0.0             |
Prepayments etc                    |  0.0             |  0.0             |  0.0             |
Stock                              |  0.0             |  0.0             |  0.0             |
Work-in-Progress                   |  0.0             |  0.0             |  0.0             |
Loans                              |  0.0             |  0.0             |  0.0             |
Tax Recoverable                    |  0.0   0.0       |  0.0   0.0       |  0.0   0.0       |
                                   |------------------|------------------|------------------|
CREDITORS DUE WITHIN ONE YEAR      |                  |                  |                  |
Bank Overdraft                     |  0.0             |  0.0             |  0.0             |
Trade Creditors & Bills            |  0.0             |  0.0             |  0.0             |
Other Creditors & Accruals         |  0.0             |  0.0             |  0.0             |
Corporation Tax (Current)          |  0.0             |  0.0             |  0.0             |
H.P. (Current)                     |  0.0             |  0.0             |  0.0             |
Other Tax & Social Security        |  0.0             |  0.0             |  0.0             |
Dividend                           |  0.0             |  0.0             |  0.0             |
Loans                              |  0.0             |  0.0             |  0.0             |
...                                |  0.0   0.0       |  0.0   0.0       |  0.0   0.0       |
-----------------------------------|------------------|------------------|------------------|
NET CURRENT ASSETS (DEFICIT)       |         0.0      |         0.0      |         0.0      |
```

Figure 4.1   Client spreadsheet (reproduced courtesy of Venture Factors PLC)

```
-------------------------------|------------------|------------------|------------------|
TOTAL ASSETS LESS CURR LIAB |        0.0 |          0.0 |          0.0 |
-------------------------------|------------------|------------------|------------------|
Due to Associated Co's      |   0.0      |   0.0      |   0.0      |
Due from Associated Co's    |   0.0    0.0 |   0.0    0.0 |   0.0    0.0 |
                            |------------------|------------------|------------------|
                            |        0.0 |          0.0 |          0.0 |
                            |------------------|------------------|------------------|
CREDITORS DUE AFTER ONE YEAR |            |            |            |
Secured Loans               |   0.0      |   0.0      |   0.0      |
Unsecured Loans             |   0.0      |   0.0      |   0.0      |
Directors Loans             |   0.0      |   0.0      |   0.0      |
Corporation Tax             |   0.0      |   0.0      |   0.0      |
H.P. (Over 1 Year)          |   0.0      |   0.0      |   0.0      |
Deferred Income             |   0.0      |   0.0      |   0.0      |
Deferred Tax                |   0.0    0.0 |   0.0    0.0 |   0.0    0.0 |
-------------------------------|------------------|------------------|------------------|
TANGIBLE NET WORTH (DEFICIT) |        0.0 |          0.0 |          0.0 |
-------------------------------|------------------|------------------|------------------|
SHAREHOLDERS FUNDS          |            |            |            |
Issued Capital              |        0.0 |          0.0 |          0.0 |
Loan Stock                  |   0.0      |   0.0      |   0.0      |
P&L Acct/Reserves           |   0.0      |   0.0      |   0.0      |
Capital Reserves            |   0.0    0.0 |   0.0    0.0 |   0.0    0.0 |
-------------------------------|------------------|------------------|------------------|
CAPITAL EMPLOYED            |        0.0 |          0.0 |          0.0 |
less Intangibles            |   0.0      |   0.0      |   0.0      |
-------------------------------|------------------|------------------|------------------|
TANGIBLE NET WORTH (DEFICIT) |        0.0 |          0.0 |          0.0 |
-------------------------------|------------------|------------------|------------------|
KEY FINANCIAL DATA and RATIOS
                            |------------------|------------------|------------------|
Turnover                    |   0.0      |   0.0      |   0.0      |
Gross Profit                |   0.0 ERROR |   0.0 ERROR |   0.0 ERROR |
Operating Profit            |   0.0 ERROR |   0.0 ERROR |   0.0 ERROR |
Pre Tax Profit              |   0.0 ERROR |   0.0 ERROR |   0.0 ERROR |
Interest Paid               |   0.0      |   0.0      |   0.0      |
Taxation                    |   0.0      |   0.0      |   0.0      |
Retained Profit             |   0.0      |   0.0      |   0.0      |
Current Assets              |   0.0      |   0.0      |   0.0      |
Current Liabilities         |   0.0      |   0.0      |   0.0      |
Net Current Assets/(Deficit)|   0.0      |   0.0      |   0.0      |
Total Interest Bearing Debt |   0.0      |   0.0      |   0.0      |
Issued Capital              |   0.0      |   0.0      |   0.0      |
Tangible Net Worth          |   0.0      |   0.0      |   0.0      |

Return on Capital Employed  | ERROR      | ERROR      | ERROR      |
Interest Cover              | ERROR times | ERROR times | ERROR times |
Debt/Equity Ratio           | ERROR :1   | ERROR :1   | ERROR :1   |
Debtor/Creditor Ratio       | ERROR :1   | ERROR :1   | ERROR :1   |
Current Ratio               | ERROR :1   | ERROR :1   | ERROR :1   |
Acid Test                   | ERROR :1   | ERROR :1   | ERROR :1   |
Working Capital Ratio       | ERROR      | ERROR      | ERROR      |
Debtor Days                 | ERROR days | ERROR days | ERROR days |
Creditor Days               | ERROR days | ERROR days | ERROR days |
Stock Turnover              | ERROR times | ERROR times | ERROR times |
Quick Cash Flow             |   0.0      |   0.0      |   0.0      |
                            |------------------|------------------|------------------|
```

Figure 4.1   Continued

including perhaps the family home, or do they undertake activities which would normally be out of character, and for example raise fraudulent invoices to the factor. Indeed, it has been quoted by a number of managers within the factoring industry that their clients 'are as honest as they can **afford** to be'.

2. The quality of the security

Factors and invoice discounters advance funds against the discounted value of an invoice. Over years of experience, factors typically advance up to 80% against approved invoices, although in recent years some have marketed their ability to advance 85% of approved invoices. There is an automatic margin of at least 20%, which acts as a cushion held against any deductions or queries in the event of the insolvency of the client company. This margin will vary directly according to the factor's perception of the potential risk of a client's customers reducing their payments to a client.

The quality of the factor's security is established from two directions:

- the quality of the debtors;
- the quality of the debt itself, i.e. the underlying collectability of the invoices.

In assessing the risks of their security, the factor asks themselves the question: 'If the client company ceases to trade for any reason, can the funds advanced be collected from the client's outstanding invoices?'

Whilst debts may have been paid effectively on an ongoing basis by a company's customers, once a supplier has ceased to trade, there is no longer an ongoing relationship and goodwill is no longer an issue. As a result, the payments performance of the customer can change markedly, with a reduction in the customer's payment to the company, or its factor, typically being seen.

The factor therefore has to assess the likelihood of its client's customers not paying in the event of their client ceasing to trade. In assessing this risk the factors ask themselves how and why payments from the failed company's customers could be 'diluted':

- Direct risks – where the features of a client's debtor book will directly reduce the amount of collectable debt for a factor.
- Indirect risks – where as a direct result of the client ceasing to trade, the client's customers reduce their payments as a result of indirect problems having been experienced through the non-continuation of supplies.

Direct risks

1. Type of product/service

The product or service being provided is crucial to the area of risk assessment. Each product and industry is different. Each will have certain nuances, which can impact upon a factor's ability to collect their funds from the client's customers in a terminal situation.

In its essence a product or service which is **buy, sell and forget** is factorable. The simpler the product, the lower the propensity for a customer to dispute an invoice, and therefore the more comfortable the factor will feel.

For example it is easier to factor a light engineering company manufacturing nuts and bolts than a heavy engineering company manufacturing and installing complex steel structures. The more complex a product, the more things can go wrong, the more chance there is of the customer disputing the outstanding invoice, especially in the event of the client company's insolvency. It is as a result of these features that the capital goods and construction industries have proven so difficult to support.

Other very difficult products to factor are those of a perishable nature, whereby the actual life of a product is very short. Problems can be seen in a terminal situation if, for example, the product quality is poor, with the goods left to rot, leaving little value to the customer who will refuse to pay for outstanding invoices.

2. Product quality

If a client company has quality problems, disputes will be seen, with the customers unlikely to pay. This creates not only a high workload for the factor chasing the outstanding debts but also compromises their ability to collect their funds in the event of client insolvency. The factor will assess a client company's commitment to quality by means of the levels of credit notes it raises to its customers.

The higher the level of disputes, the higher the level of credit notes that will be raised to offset the financial constraint that disputes present and the lower the level of funds advanced. Typically any percentage points of credit notes over 3% of turnover are taken directly off the standard advance rate offered to a particular industry. For example, if credit notes amount to 5% it is likely the incoming factors would seek to reduce their maximum funding levels to 75% of invoice value.[3]

As companies approach insolvency the desire to get goods or services to their customers as quickly as possible to raise invoices to generate cash from the factor becomes paramount, so quality can typically become a secondary issue. This further increases the risks of dispute, and compromises the factor's ability to collect out their funds in a terminal situation. Thus if credit note levels are high, the factor effectively doubles the level of credit notes seen to generate an approximation of the likely levels of 'dilution' of their security upon insolvency.

3. Quality of the client's customers

The quality of the client company's customer base is essential to the factor. If a client's customer ceases to trade, the debt with that particular customer has no value to the factor. If the client company has insufficient reserves to cope with a bad debt and ceases to trade at the same time, the factor has an uncollectable debt, reducing its security, increasing the potential for a client bad debt.

The better the creditworthiness of the customers the more likely they are to have the financial ability to pay for the goods or services provided. Conversely, the lower the quality of customers the more chance of insolvencies being seen and the factor's security compromised. Weaker customers are also the most likely to generate spurious disputes as a smoke screen to defer and even refuse payment to a factor collecting out their security.

The standard proposal form in Figure 4.2 is taken from Griffin Factors Ltd and highlights that the factor will look at the quality of the top ten customers, to get a 'feel' for the overall customer quality. The factor will also note the levels of bad debt experienced over the past three years to see how the quality of customers has been, how effectively the client has managed their credit control and how the bad debts have impacted upon the client's profitability.

The lower the quality of customers, the less likely the factor is to provide facilities to the client. Indeed, if they did support a client who had weak customers it is likely they would seek to advance lower levels of funds.

4. Customer type/location

In addition to the customer quality the type of customer needs to be taken into consideration. For example there are logistical problems in chasing night-clubs and pubs owing to the unsociable opening hours. Equally if the client's customers are located in difficult areas, which are experiencing their own internal difficulties, for instance certain areas within the Middle East or central Africa, the factor may decline support.

5. Satisfactory order/invoice cycle

Factors wish to establish a clear 'order/invoice' cycle, which shows goods or services have been delivered against a given order, usually supported by some proof of completion of the service or delivery, e.g. proof of deliveries for goods, signed time sheets, satisfaction notes, and so on. It is essential that the goods or services have been delivered to the customer with confirmation received thereto. If the factor seeks to enforce payment and the products have not been produced in accordance with a given order or if they have not been received, the customer will dispute the invoice and the factor has an uncollectable debt. This issue becomes critical in the event of the supplier's demise, as the factor will need supportive paperwork to disprove spurious disputes that always materialise in a terminal situation.

COMPANY INFORMATION

Name of organisation _____

Address _____

Postcode _____

Telephone _____ Name of contact _____

PRODUCT INFORMATION

Please describe briefly the
products or services that your
business supplies _____

STATUTORY INFORMATION

Company registered number _____

Registered office _____

Date established _____ Issued share capital £ _____

DIRECTORS/PARTNERS

1 First names _____ Surname _____

Address _____

Postcode _____ Bank sort code _____ Shares held _____

2 First names _____ Surname _____

Address _____

Postcode _____ Bank sort code _____ Shares held _____

3 First names _____ Surname _____

Address _____

Postcode _____ Bank sort code _____ Shares held _____

4 First names _____ Surname _____

Address _____

Postcode _____ Bank sort code _____ Shares held _____

Have any of the above named
been associated with a
business that has failed?
Please give details. _____

OTHER SHAREHOLDERS

1 First names _____ Surname _____

Address _____

Postcode _____ Shares held _____

2 First names _____ Surname _____

Address _____

Postcode _____ Shares held _____

(a)

Figure 4.2 Proposal form (reproduced courtesy of Griffin Factors)

ASSOCIATE COMPANIES

Please give names and registration numbers of any associate companies, including parent or subsidiary

FINANCIAL INFORMATION

Bankers

Address

Postcode

Bank sort code   *Max balance (last three months) £*

Overdraft facility   *Interest rate*   %

Current balance £   *Security held*

Other facilities/loans:

1

Name

Balance outstanding £   *Type of loan*

Security held

2

Name

Balance outstanding £   *Type of loan*

Security held

Trading results

	Turnover (Gross)	Pre-tax profit	Bad debts
Last year	£	£	£
Current year	£	£	£
Projected next year	£	£	£

Do you have a credit insurance policy?   Yes ☐   No ☐   *(Please tick as appropriate)*

If yes, please give details

CREDITOR INFORMATION

Please state amounts currently outstanding in respect of   VAT £   PAYE £

Please list your two principle suppliers (they will not be contacted), detailing:

1

Name

Goods purchased   *Average purchases per month £*

Payment terms   *Current balance £*

2

Name

Goods purchased   *Average purchases per month £*

Payment terms   *Current balance £*

Please state the total balance of your purchase ledger currently outstanding £

(b)

Figure 4.2   Continued

Number of customer accounts	Active over last 12 months			Active now	

Types of customer (% of total)	Trade (UK)		%	Local Authority/Government		%
	Export including Eire		%	General public		%

Do you anticipate sales to any one customer will exceed 30% of total annual sales?

Yes ☐ No ☐ *(Please tick as appropriate)*

If yes, please specify _____

Please specify your standard terms of trade, including any settlement discounts offered (as per invoice)

If you offer any customers special terms, please give details

Detail your eight principal customers (they will not be contacted) who have the highest credit sales

1
Full company name
Company registration no.
Address
Bank sort code _____ Required credit limit £ _____

2
Full company name
Company registration no.
Address
Bank sort code _____ Required credit limit £ _____

3
Full company name
Company registration no.
Address
Bank sort code _____ Required credit limit £ _____

4
Full company name
Company registration no.
Address
Bank sort code _____ Required credit limit £ _____

5
Full company name
Company registration no.
Address
Bank sort code _____ Required credit limit £ _____

6
Full company name
Company registration no.
Address
Bank sort code _____ Required credit limit £ _____

7
Full company name
Company registration no.
Address
Bank sort code _____ Required credit limit £ _____

8
Full company name
Company registration no.
Address
Bank sort code _____ Required credit limit £ _____

(c)

Figure 4.2 Continued

SALES ANALYSIS

What proportion of your sales involve	Sale or return .... %		Work in progress .... %	
	Invoicing before delivery .... %		Associate companies .... %	
	Retentions* .... %		Forward dating of invoices .... %	
	Free issue material† .... %		Sales to your suppliers .... %	

*Witholding of agreed percentage of sums due until product/service performance is proved satisfactory.   †Materials provided by your customers for processing.

Please give details of your sales over the last 12 months	*Month*	*Number of invoices*	*Value of invoices (incl VAT)*	*Number of credit notes*	*Value of credit notes (incl VAT)*
			£		£
			£		£
			£		£
			£		£
			£		£
			£		£
			£		£
			£		£
			£		£
			£		£
			£		£
			£		£
Totals			£		£

Total of debtors outstanding at last month end   Number ....   Value £ ....

ADDITIONAL INFORMATION REQUIRED

Please enclose the following when returning this proposal form
- **Last audited accounts and any subsequent management information**
- **Sales literature**
- **Sample invoice and credit note**
- **Conditions of sale**
- **Copy of customer list with balances (aged if possible)**
- **Month end debtor figures**

DECLARATION

I/We declare that the information given is correct to the best of my/our knowledge. I/We am/are not aware of any adverse information which I/we have not disclosed to you which might influence your decision.   Signature ....   Position in Company ....   Date ....

Please return to your local office. Addresses listed overleaf.
If you require further assistance with your application please contact
your local business development manager.

(d)

Figure 4.2 Continued

Without clear evidence that the goods or service have been effectively delivered, the factor will feel highly exposed and without agreement to change systems, may not support a company.

6. Terms of trade

Terms of trade vary markedly from industry to industry, which renders certain industries more appropriate to factoring than others. Certain terms which cannot be supported by factors, are shown in Table 4.2.

Table 4.2 Standard terms of trade that cannot be financed by factors, with solutions if applicable

Term description	Implications for the factor in a terminal situation	Possible solutions
Sale or return	The goods can be returned, which will render an invoice valueless.	Cannot be financed.
Consignment sales/ pay when sold	Goods are held on the client's premises to the order of a customer, being called off as and when they are needed. In the event of insolvency, there will be a question mark over whether the goods supplied represent stocks or debtors. If a receiver is appointed, they will have title to the client's stock but not their debtors. As a result, they may seek to realise the value of the stock at the factor's expense.	If the goods are stored separately and clearly marked as the property of the customer, with the factor's interest duly noted, some factors may support this type of debt, providing it is a small percentage of the business.
Extended terms	To overcome a difficult seasonal period in a company's working capital cycle, extended terms may be offered, e.g. caravan sales and garden products can be 180 days during the winter months. The longer the terms, the greater the risk of customer insolvency and the risk of problems arising with the products themselves.	During the months where extended terms are offered, subject to the customers being credit-worthy, the level of finance advanced could be reduced, reverting to the standard levels of finance when standard credit terms apply.
Stage payments	To ease the cash flow cycle on larger transactions stage payments may be requested. If the supplier fails, the work will not be completed and the outstanding invoices may be subject to dispute.	Providing the customer will sign confirmation that the completion of other stages does not impact upon the payment for the current stage, some factors may provide limited support.
Invoicing in advance	In certain industries some services may be provided over a protracted period of time, but paid in advance, e.g. maintenance	Cannot be financed.

Table 4.2   Continued

	contracts for computers are typically paid for a 12-month period and invoiced upfront. Clearly in a terminal situation a customer will not pay for the service if it has not been delivered.	
Contra trading (or reciprocal trading)	When a client company's customer is also a client's supplier, a conflict can exist. Should the client company cease to trade, their customer will withhold the payment due to them.	Generally, these accounts will be excluded. However, if the amount owed by the customer is substantially more than the amount owing to the customer, the factor may accept the account at reduced funding. They will require an aged creditors analysis to be submitted every month. The liability on the purchase ledger would then be deducted from the invoice value to the customer for funding purposes.
Free issue material	In certain industries goods may be provided to the client company by a customer for a value added service to be provided, e.g. lamination services to trade printers. In the event of client failure, if the customer is unable to retrieve their goods, they will seek to offset the cost of their goods against any outstanding invoices for the value added service which the factor holds as part of its security	If the levels of free issue material is small, say 5% of sales value, then the factors may live with it. More than this will cause them to reappraise their funding considerations and looking towards reducing their advance rate.
Tooling	In the engineering industry, a customer may be invoiced for a bespoke tool as well as the final product produced. The tool may remain with the client but remain the property of the customer. Upon insolvency, the customer will not have immediate access to their tool and may seek to deduct both the value of the tool and loss of profits against existing outstanding invoices.	This can be very hard to finance, and if the values are high the client will not be supported.
Cash deposits	If deposits are taken upfront on a regular basis, the customer will seek to offset the value of any deposits held by the supplier against any invoices from the supplier.	If the values are small, the factor may support, albeit at a lower percentage advance rate.
Retentions	Prevalent within the construction industry, say 5%/6 months. Retentions will not be paid in the event of a supplier failing until the contractual time of the retention has elapsed.	Retentions need to be invoiced separately when they fall due for payment.

7. Contractual conflicts

The factor needs to be certain that they have clear title to the invoices against which they are providing finance. Six principal conflicts exist:

1. A bank's previous debenture/fixed and floating charge which includes the company's book debts – a letter of waiver needs to be obtained from the bank's debenture before a factor has clear title. By so doing, it is likely the level of finance being provided by the bank will be reduced, as part of its security will have been lost to another financial institution.[4]
2. A ban on assignment – these terms of trade tend to be included within many local authority and construction related contracts. Whilst typically designed to restrict the contract itself being sub-contracted to a third party, a waiver needs to be obtained from the necessary parties to allow the client's debts to be assigned to the factor, thereby giving the factor clear title to the debts created as a result of the contract.
3. Retention of title (ROT) – ROT in itself is an extensive subject and has been the focus of attention by many specialist lawyers. With so few actual legal precedents established in regards ROT, factors and other financiers err on the side of caution when considering any ROT clauses. Some ROT clauses extend the retention of title to the products supplied through to the client company's customers themselves. In a terminal situation, the client's supplier may recourse to their terms and conditions and collect their goods back from the end customer, compromising the factor's ability to collect the outstanding balance. If major suppliers have tight extended ROT clauses, a client will be required to obtain a specific letter of waiver prior to the factor financing those debts.
4. Building and construction related contracts – JCT.80 contracts, 'pay as paid' contracts and other contracts of a construction nature are, with very rare exceptions, unable to be financed by a factor. Too often onerous clauses exist within the construction sector – contracts for liquidated damages, the withholding of taxation via 714 certificates, payments against interim valuations, and so on. These terms may result in the customer refusing to pay for a client's given invoices in a terminal situation, although the work may have been carried out effectively by the client company.[5]
5. Ongoing contracts – an underlying contract may specify the supply of product over a given period of time. In the event of the client company's demise it is unable to fulfil a given contract, with a customer potentially seeking to offset any additional costs from outstanding invoices.
6. Extended warranties – for certain products, e.g. white goods (where warranties beyond 12 months may be offered) and casement windows (where 10 year guarantees may be offered), these can compromise a factor's position. Given a supplier no longer trades, the warranty has no value, with offset against a factored client's outstanding invoices likely.

The above risks can be minimised in certain circumstances by negotiation, with specific waivers drawn up to ensure unencumbered title exists, enabling the factor to provide finance.

Indirect risks

1. Spread of the customer base

Factors like to see their risk diversified. Accordingly, a factor likes to see a good spread of customers within the client's debtor book. Typically, they would prefer not to see the major customer forming more than 20–30% of the outstanding receivables.

A client company's reliance upon a major customer representing more than say 50% of the outstanding sales ledger, can present increased risks to a factor:

● Should the customer cease to trade, the factor's security is directly reduced by the amount of outstanding debts.
● The client company can become dangerously dependent upon the major customer for the survival of the business itself. If the client's customer switched suppliers, there is a danger of insolvency occurring, as the client company may have geared up their overheads to satisfy that customer.
● Should the whole of the customer's account be disputed, the factor is highly vulnerable.
● Fraud – should a client decide to attempt to defraud a factor via a variety of methods, the factor has a valueless debt. If the fraud is perpetrated using the major customer, the factor is exposed to greater risk and could experience substantial loss.

Whilst the issue of a poor spread of customers does present increased risks to the factoring industry in general, there are certain factors and a number of merchant financiers (Chapter 3) who may be able to assist. In these cases, they require very tight underlying paperwork, which may include signed acceptance of the quality, together with credit insurance being put in place against the customer. As a result, the fees charged tend to be higher, but their argument is simple – 'risk versus reward'.

2. Ageing of the debts

An old debt is a cold debt.

A useful but true adage from the credit control manuals. The older the debts, the more the chance there is something wrong with them and the less the level of finance made available by the factor.

Recourse factors, i.e. those who do not provide bad debt protection, will typically finance debts up to 90 days past the due date.[6] After this date, the debts will either be reassigned back, in other words returned to the company for them to chase the outstanding debt, absolving the factor of any responsibilities, or subject to an additional 'refactoring charge' of around 0.5–1% of the outstanding value to the client company. This charge is debited to the client's account, and represents the extra administration costs required to continue chasing the debt.

3. Single supplier

Again, looking to diversify their risks, factors do not feel comfortable with a client company relying upon a single supplier. If the client company has only one major supplier, supporting the business, and that supplier fails, the factors may have to collect out their security, as their client is equally likely to fail.

Another major concern relating to the single supplier, is that if the supplier encounters product quality, the client will be selling poor quality goods into the marketplace, which will result in a high incidence of quality disputes and the factors having extreme difficulties in recouping their monies in the event of the client's subsequent demise.

Contingent risks

1. The underlying contract

Although a company may have 'blue chip' debtors, who may have the financial resources to comfortably pay an outstanding debt, if they will be faced with extra costs of having a specific contract completed as a result of a supplier's demise, the customer may seek to 'offset' any additional costs incurred against the debts owed to the supplier and their factor.

Consider for example a contract for the refurbishment of council houses. Suppose a construction company successfully tendered for a £350k fixed price contract to refurbish 250 council houses. Whilst each house will be refurbished individually, should the company cease to trade after having completed 150 houses, and invoicing £210k, the council will be required to go into the marketplace to get another contractor to complete the contract. Now only having 100 houses to refurbish as compared to the original 250, the new contractor will not be able to benefit from the same economies of scale as compared to the original contract.

Given that the new contractor tenders at, say, £200k, the total cost to the council for the whole project will now be £210k + £200k, i.e. £410k. As a result, the costs to the council are likely to be higher by some £60k. With the current culture within the public sector, it is likely the additional costs will be offset against the invoices owed to the original contractor. If this contractor was, however, factoring, this offset would be seen by the factor who would experience loss.

2. Contra accounts/reciprocal trading

If a customer also acts as a supplier, whilst on an ongoing basis debts may be paid effectively by both parties by an exchange of cheques or by contra, in a terminal situation the 'contra' may be offset against any outstanding invoices. Once a supplier has ceased to trade, there is no longer an ongoing relationship. With the benefits of an ongoing relationship no longer present the payments performance of the customer will change markedly, with the customer's payment to the company, or its factor, being reduced to reflect the funds they are owed.

3. Fraud

One of the major contingent risks to the factor is that of fraud. Whilst very few clients actually commence factoring with the intention of defrauding the factor, fraudulent activity most typically stems from the client management's desperate attempt to save their business. Whilst many may believe their attempts at fraud to be unique, the majority of frauds fall into the following areas:

- Pre-invoicing – raising an invoice prior to the goods being shipped in an attempt to generate cash at an earlier point in time.
- 'Fresh-air' invoicing – raising an invoice against which no goods or services have been supplied.
- Banking of monies owed to the factor – monies due to the factor but paid and banked to their own account by the client. This represents a 'cardinal sin' within the factoring industry and even if innocent can result in immediate termination of the agreement.
- Deliberate delay in the raising of credit notes. Credit notes reduce the level of finance available from the factor. Delaying the issue of credit notes, maintains the level of finance available from the factor, until it is too late.

3. The quality of the management

The final area of consideration is consistent with almost all financial transactions – do the management have the necessary skills to achieve what they are setting out to do?

The assessment of management skills is highly subjective and depends upon the individual sales manager's or account manager's 'gut feel' as to the management's capabilities. Typically, CVs are examined to establish the management's track record and ability to perform.

Personal credit searches are undertaken on the company directors/partners, and some factors even seek personal banker's references. How the directors handle their own credit can reflect how they will handle the credit offered by the factor, and indeed a number of factors will refuse support if they discover

County Court Judgements against directors, unless there is good reason for them and that the judgements have been fully satisfied by the respective court.

Additionally, the factors will examine any past business history that the client management has had. Whilst not automatically refusing to support a client company whose management has had a previous business failure, they will seek to get full information regarding the previous business.

Companies house will show any directorships the client management has had and investigations are carried out in full.[7]

Rating systems

A number of the factoring and invoice discounting houses have devised 'rating systems' to assess the risks associated with their clients. Similar to the bond and bank rating systems, each client is classified according to the two principal areas of risk:

- the quality of security
- the financial performance.

A client will be given a score according to the collectability of the security, and the financial performance of the client company. In this way, if a client company has a specific need, a decision maker can get a quick 'feel' for the client by looking at their rating. This can assist with their decision making capability, in the absence of the manager responsible for the day-to-day handling of that particular client.

Some factors apportion a numeric or alphabetical rating to both areas. With an A to E rating system, if a client has a rating of AA, it is easier to make a positive decision than a client holding a DD rating, where some doubt might be expressed as to the quality of the security and the client's financial position.

Additional security

As described earlier, the factors will seek to recoup their funds from the client's customers if the client fails. However, as a company heads towards insolvency it can become harder to collect outstanding funds. As a result, the factors need to be able to rely upon the existing client management providing support to assist them in collecting their funds, to resolve spurious disputes, etc. To this end, personal guarantees are usually sought to support the factors' agreement, dependent upon the strength of the overall proposition.

Although not typically supported by a charge over personal assets, the personal guarantee extends to any liability that remains to the factor in the event of them not being able to collect out their funds from the client's invoices. This guarantee could technically extend to the total value of funds advanced to the client company.

Theoretically if a client supplies goods of merchantable quality in accordance with customers' purchase orders and delivers them to good quality customers on time, invoices should be paid in the event of the client's insolvency and no liability should remain. Thus if the invoices received by the factor are supported by good quality paperwork the chances of a factor needing recourse to the guarantors of an agreement are minimised. Guarantees are generally taken in order to secure the client management's support in helping the factor to collect out their funds if the client company fails. If a guarantee is in place, there is a financial incentive to the client management in assisting the factors in their collection of funds.

Some factors are able to consider performance warranties, which are more geared towards ensuring the agreement is adhered to and that no fraudulent activity is perpetrated. Equally, some factors may be able to restrict the personal guarantee to a known value, rather than making it unlimited, although these issues form part of the negotiation process, and are dependent upon how the overall strength of the financing proposition.

In marginal cases, the factor may also seek to take residual security over other assets, especially if the factoring facility is required to replace an existing overdraft facility.

Under confidential invoice discounting facilities, a fixed charge over book debts or an all assets debenture will always be taken over a client company. This is to avoid a client company seeking to discount the same sales ledger twice. For under a CID facility, the client's customers are not aware of the discounter's involvement. The security taken is registered at companies house, information of which is available to any other potential invoice discounter undertaking their due diligence.

Note of caution

Those readers who may be assessing a factoring or discounting option are strongly advised to seek professional legal advice before signing any personal guarantees, warranties and agreements with factoring companies.

Summary

As we have seen, factors are making serious efforts to dispense with the historic tag of 'last resort finance', with this attitude duly reflected in their close appraisal of a potential client's financial position. Although we have sought to outline the negative views that factors take over certain situations, it should be noted that some of the more commercial factors will support companies in some of the above potentially difficult situations, providing other areas, such as profitability and financial stability, are good, although they may seek to take additional security to manage their risks more effectively, and seek to charge a premium for providing these services.

NOTES

1 Usually, revaluation reserves for property are excluded from tangible net worth as are any intangible balance sheet items, e.g. goodwill. Typically, directors' loans, if subordinated (i.e. where agreement is held not to withdraw the funds from the business without the consent of the factor), can be viewed as 'quasi-capital'.

2 For example a temporary recruitment agency would be expected to have a debt turn of between 30–45 days, whilst a printer may be expected to have between 75–90 days.

3 Traditionally, this explains why textiles and clothing companies generally receive a maximum of 75% funding. In this industry returns tend to be fairly high with quality typically inconsistent. Credit note levels of 5–7.5% of turnover are not untypical.

4 It is essential for a potential factoring client to ascertain their banker's reaction to them factoring – to evaluate fully the net benefit factoring will bring.

5 One example we have assisted with was a temporary manpower agency to the construction sector. Their previously very successful company failed as a result of them working under a 'pay as paid' contract. Their customer accounted for around 40% of their business and was of good financial standing. Their customer, however, was one of the main contractors to Olympia and York. The contractor did not get paid and relied upon their 'pay as paid' contract to withhold payment to the client company, which failed as a direct result.

6 It should, however, be noted that some recourse factors will only finance debts up to 60 days past due.

7 In our experience, it is advisable to inform the factors of any previous adverse credit history when having discussions with them. We have seen a number of companies have their factoring facilities terminated when some adverse credit information materialised of which the management deliberately sought to hide at the time due diligence was undertaken.

Chapter 5

The factoring facility: the costs

There are a number of myths surrounding the actual costs of factoring and invoice discounting, ranging from the glib remark of 'factoring is expensive', through to the misconception that the factor advances 80% of an invoice and keeps the rest as their charges.

In reality two direct charges are incurred by factoring and discounting clients:

● administration costs – expressed as a percentage of gross turnover, and
● the cost of funds expressed as a percentage over bank base rates.

FACTORING

The factoring service provides the following:

● sales ledger administration
● full credit control
● credit information
● credit protection (non-recourse facilities only).

Administration costs

The administration costs will vary according to the workload the factoring company anticipates in relation to the volumes of turnover they expect to see. In assessing the pricing of a facility, three key features are examined:

1. The level of turnover

The administration income generated by the factor is directly related to gross turnover, with their fees being charged as a percentage of gross turnover. The higher the level of turnover, the higher the earning capacity of the factor and the lower the percentage administration fee. At the lower end of the turnover range, £100k, administration fees of 3–3.5% are not untypical, whereas beyond turnover levels of around £2m, a reasonable overhead contribution is received by the factors, who can fine-tune their pricing as a result.

2. The number of active accounts

The more customers the factor is required to chase for outstanding payments, the greater the variable costs incurred – monthly statements, telephone calls, chasing letters, etc. As the workload increases, the more expensive the facility becomes.

3. The number of invoices and credit notes

The factor has to process all the invoices and credit notes the client company raises. The greater the number of invoices, the greater the costs incurred. Typically, in assessing the issue of price, a factor will look at the current average invoice value size to gauge how many invoices will be processed over the coming year.

As an indication of costs profiles and how they change, compare the three examples in Table 5.1. We can see from this table that the higher the level of turnover, the lower the actual % charged to the client. On a pro rata basis the high workload accounts, where the average invoice value is low and the number of customers is high, are proportionally more expensive.

Table 5.1 Examples of costing profile and how they change

	ABC Ltd	DEF Ltd	ABC Ltd	DEF Ltd	ABC Ltd	DEF Ltd
Net turnover	£100k	£100k	£1m	£1m	£4m	£4m
Average invoice value	£500	£2500	£500	£2500	£500	£2500
Active customers	20	4	195	40	780	160
Approximate fee structure	3.9%	3.3%	1.49%	0.88%	1.3%	0.68%
Annual admin. costs	£4.6k	£3.9k	£17.5k	£10.3k	£60.7k	£31.9k
Approximate level of funds advanced	£10k	£10k	£100k	£100k	£400k	£400k
Cost of funds (over bank base rates)	3%	3%	2.5%	2.5%	2%	2%
Actual annual finance costs (assuming bank base rate of 6%)	£900	£900	£8500	£8500	£32 000	£32 000
Total projected annual costs of the facility	£5.4k	£4.8k	£26k	£18.8k	£92.7k	£63.9k

In extreme circumstances, where the proposal involves a very high work-load, factoring can prove unviable, for example in the case of a company manufacturing and distributing contact lenses who were looking for cash flow funding.

Their customers were independent opticians who would typically place orders to the value of £50. The client had in the region of 300 customers and was projecting about £1m turnover for their first year. They received provisional estimates of cost of administration ranging between 5–7.5%, an unviable proposition. A package was finally arranged with a commercial recourse factor where the client would actively chase the smaller accounts directly, whilst the factor chased the larger accounts, but maintaining control over the facility by sending out monthly statements and chasing letters. As a result, the fee structure was reduced to 3.65%.

The cost of funds

The factors are typically backed by financial institutions, and act as a wholesaler of money for their main distributors, their parent banks. The cost of funds from their parent banks, by the very nature of the borrowing must generate a profit for the parent banks. As a result, the costs of funds to the factor will be higher than in the standard banking market.

Anecdotal discussions seem to suggest the cost of funds to the factors vary between 1% and 1.6% over base for mainstream factors and discounters, and the figures are higher for the smaller independent factors.

Usually, the cost of funds charged to a client will reflect the perceived risks and the likely level of competitive pressure that exists for the client's business. The cost of funds, however, can have a 'machismo' effect, i.e. the lower the rate charges, the lower the perceived risk. As a result, many people when negotiating a factoring or discounting package tend to focus upon the cost of funds.

Some factors use this to their advantage, as the reduced cost of funds has a high perceived value. The actual cost of funds is not the key expense in a factoring or a discounting package. Consider the following:

A company turns over £2m (gross) and expects its debts to be collected in 60 days. The company is looking to draw an average of £250k of funds from its factor and has been offered a facility at the cost structure given in Table 5.2.

Table 5.2 Sample cost structure

		Annual costs
Administration rate	0.85%	£17 000
Cost of funds	2.5%	£21 250 (assuming base rates of 6%)
Total costs		£39 250

In negotiating the facility, if the client company can negotiate a saving of 0.05% off its administration rate, to 0.8%, an annual saving of £1000 on the administration costs will be achieved. This £1000 saving compares directly to a reduction in the costs of funds of 0.4%, from 2.5% to 2.1% over base.

The perceived reduction in the costs of funds appears substantially more, although both have the same financial result.

Table 5.3 is designed to assist a potential factoring client to assess where the true costs of the facility lie.

Table 5.3 Monetary savings from changes in administration and funding costs

				Administration charges						
Turnover (gross)	0.05%	0.10%	0.15%	0.20%	0.25%	0.30%	0.35%	0.40%	0.45%	0.50%
£500 000	£250	£500	£750	£1 000	£1 250	£1 500	£1 750	£2 000	£2 250	£2 500
£1 000 000	£500	£1 000	£1 500	£2 000	£2 500	£3 000	£3 500	£4 000	£4 500	£5 000
£1 500 000	£750	£1 500	£2 250	£3 000	£3 750	£4 500	£5 250	£6 000	£6 750	£7 500
£2 000 000	£1 000	£2 000	£3 000	£4 000	£5 000	£6 000	£7 000	£8 000	£9 000	£10 000
£2 500 000	£1 250	£2 500	£3 750	£5 000	£6 250	£7 500	£8 750	£10 000	£11 250	£12 500
£3 000 000	£1 500	£3 000	£4 500	£6 000	£7 500	£9 000	£10 500	£12 000	£13 500	£15 000
£3 500 000	£1 750	£3 500	£5 250	£7 000	£8 750	£10 500	£12 250	£14 000	£15 750	£17 500
£4 000 000	£2 000	£4 000	£6 000	£8 000	£10 000	£12 000	£14 000	£16 000	£18 000	£20 000
£4 500 000	£2 250	£4 500	£6 750	£9 000	£11 250	£13 500	£15 750	£18 000	£20 250	£22 500
£5 000 000	£2 500	£5 000	£7 500	£10 000	£12 500	£15 000	£17 500	£20 000	£22 500	£25 000
£5 500 000	£2 750	£5 500	£8 250	£11 000	£13 750	£16 500	£19 250	£22 000	£24 750	£27 500
£6 000 000	£3 000	£6 000	£9 000	£12 000	£15 000	£18 000	£21 000	£24 000	£27 000	£30 000
£6 500 000	£3 250	£6 500	£9 750	£13 000	£16 250	£19 500	£22 750	£26 000	£29 250	£32 500
£7 000 000	£3 500	£7 000	£10 500	£14 000	£17 500	£21 000	£24 500	£28 000	£31 500	£35 000
£7 500 000	£3 750	£7 500	£11 250	£15 000	£18 750	£22 500	£26 250	£30 000	£33 750	£37 500
£8 000 000	£4 000	£8 000	£12 000	£16 000	£20 000	£24 000	£28 000	£32 000	£36 000	£40 000
£8 500 000	£4 250	£8 500	£12 750	£17 000	£21 250	£25 500	£29 750	£34 000	£38 250	£42 500
£9 000 000	£4 500	£9 000	£13 500	£18 000	£22 500	£27 000	£31 500	£36 000	£40 500	£45 000
£9 500 000	£4 750	£9 500	£14 250	£19 000	£23 750	£28 500	£33 250	£38 000	£42 750	£47 500
£10 000 000	£5 000	£10 000	£15 000	£20 000	£25 000	£30 000	£35 000	£40 000	£45 000	£50 000

				Cost of funds						
	0.10%	0.20%	0.30%	0.40%	0.50%	0.60%	0.70%	0.80%	0.90%	1.00%
£50 000	£50	£100	£150	£200	£250	£300	£350	£400	£450	£500
£100 000	£100	£200	£300	£400	£500	£600	£700	£800	£900	£1 000
£150 000	£150	£300	£450	£600	£750	£900	£1 050	£1 200	£1 350	£1 500
£200 000	£200	£400	£600	£800	£1 000	£1 200	£1 400	£1 600	£1 800	£2 000
£250 000	£250	£500	£750	£1 000	£1 250	£1 500	£1 750	£2 000	£2 250	£2 500
£300 000	£300	£600	£900	£1 200	£1 500	£1 800	£2 100	£2 400	£2 700	£3 000
£350 000	£350	£700	£1 050	£1 400	£1 750	£2 100	£2 450	£2 800	£3 150	£3 500
£400 000	£400	£800	£1 200	£1 600	£2 000	£2 400	£2 800	£3 200	£3 600	£4 000
£450 000	£450	£900	£1 350	£1 800	£2 250	£2 700	£3 150	£3 600	£4 050	£4 500
£500 000	£500	£1 000	£1 500	£2 000	£2 500	£3 000	£3 500	£4 000	£4 500	£5 000
£550 000	£550	£1 100	£1 650	£2 200	£2 750	£3 300	£3 850	£4 400	£4 950	£5 500
£600 000	£600	£1 200	£1 800	£2 400	£3 000	£3 600	£4 200	£4 800	£5 400	£6 000
£650 000	£650	£1 300	£1 950	£2 600	£3 250	£3 900	£4 550	£5 200	£5 850	£6 500
£700 000	£700	£1 400	£2 100	£2 800	£3 500	£4 200	£4 900	£5 600	£6 300	£7 000
£750 000	£750	£1 500	£2 250	£3 000	£3 750	£4 500	£5 250	£6 000	£6 750	£7 500
£800 000	£800	£1 600	£2 400	£3 200	£4 000	£4 800	£5 600	£6 400	£7 200	£8 000
£850 000	£850	£1 700	£2 550	£3 400	£4 250	£5 100	£5 950	£6 800	£7 650	£8 500
£900 000	£900	£1 800	£2 700	£3 600	£4 500	£5 400	£6 300	£7 200	£8 100	£9 000
£950 000	£950	£1 900	£2 850	£3 800	£4 750	£5 700	£6 650	£7 600	£8 550	£9 500
£1 000 000	£1 000	£2 000	£3 000	£4 000	£5 000	£6 000	£7 000	£8 000	£9 000	£10 000

Bad debt protection premiums

The premiums for bad debt protection will vary according to:

● the client's industry

● the client's bad debt history.

With most of the factors who provide bad debt protection, the under-writing is carried out in-house[1] with the losses equally taken in-house as well. As a result, in assessing the premiums, as with any form of insurance, the risks of bad debts need to be closely assessed. Industry sectors are examined closely, to see the incidence of bad debts, together with the client's own experience. For example, the construction industry is viewed more cynically than others, with the premium reflected accordingly.

Typically, the bad debt premiums charged by the factors vary between 0.3% and 0.6% (again charged on gross turnover).

Minimum incomes

The majority of factoring and discounting agreements have a 'minimum income' clause. This reflects the necessary income a factor needs to generate to cover the actual projected costs of running a facility. With a client's costing profile principally being determined by their level of turnover, the factor's fees are very sensitive to changing turnover levels. Thus if a percentage fee is negotiated upon the basis of a client's projected level of turnover, and the actual turnover level falls substantially short of this target, the level of fees generated by the factor may not cover the costs of running the facility. The minimum income protects the factor from this eventuality.

Typically, the minimum income figure is established by evaluating the total projected administration income the factor believes they will generate, and multiplying this by a multiple of 70%.

For instance, if a company is factoring and has £1m gross turnover and is expecting to pay 1% in administration income to the factor, the expected annual income to be generated would be £10 000. The factor would seek a minimum level of income of around £7000. If over the next 12 months the level of sales fell short of the projected level, say £500k (gross), the factor will have generated £5k of fees, some £2k below their minimum income level of £7k. The factor would then debit the shortfall of £2K to the client's account.

Typical costs – factoring

Table 5.4 Summary of the typical costs for factoring facilities

Services provided	Recourse factoring	Non-recourse factoring
Finance	✓	✓
Sales ledger administration	✓	✓
Credit control	✓	✓
Bad debt protection	✗	✓
Disclosure to the customer	✓	✓
Finance (over bank base rates)	2–3.5%	2–3.5%
Administration charges	0.35–3.5%	0.5–3.5%
Bad debt protection	N/A	included
Minimum fixed costs (p.a.)	from £1750	from £3000

INVOICE DISCOUNTING

The costing structure for an invoice discounting facility is similar to that for factoring, although with the clients maintaining control of their own sales ledgers. However, the administration fees are markedly lower.

The administration fees charged by the discounter cover the costs of monitoring the client's sales ledger, together with the regular audits undertaken on the client's premises validating their security. They will usually also include the bank charges incurred by the factor in running the trust account held on behalf of the client, although as margins come under increasing pressure, it is likely that bank charges will begin to be charged separately.

As with the majority of financial institutions, the factor/discounter needs to obtain a return on their capital employed and tend to evaluate their costings on the basis of the yield they can generate on the finance advanced to their client, revising their costs according to the perceived risks.

For example, consider a company turning over £2m and collecting its debts in 60 days which has an average outstanding sales ledger of £386.3k. The maximum draw down, given a net funding line of 70% (after reserves withheld by the discounter), would generate about £270k. Given the likely average level of usage was £250k, and the likely costs of money to the client of 2.5% over base for funds advanced. The discounter evaluates their returns as shown in Table 5.5.

The yield required will reflect the perceived risks – the risk/reward ratio. The lower the risks, the lower the yield the invoice discounter requires. As a result of the discounter's evaluation of yield, if a potential client requires less than full funding, they should be able to negotiate their fee structure downwards – less funds = less risk. (Table 5.6.)

Table 5.5 Evaluation of funding structure by invoice discounters

Administration fee (on gross turnover) (%)	Costs (£)	Percentage yield on projected average finance (£250k)	Effective cost of funds (expressed as rate over base including 2.5%) (%)
0.45	10 579	4.23	6.73
0.4	9 400	3.8	6.3
0.35	8 225	3.3	5.8
0.3	7 050	2.8	5.3
0.25	5 875	2.4	4.9

Table 5.6 Typical charges – invoice discounting

Services and costs	Disclosed invoice discounting	Confidential invoice discounting
Finance	✓	✓
Sales ledger administration	✗	✗
Credit control	✗	✗
Bad debt protection*	optional	optional
Disclosure to the customer	✓	✗
Administration charges	0.25–1%	0.1–0.75%
Finance (over bank base rates)	2–3%	1.75–3%
including bad debt protection	0.65–1.5%	0.5–1.25%
Minimum fixed costs (p.a.)	c. £5000	c. £6000

* Most discounters will take assignment to an existing credit insurance policy if already in place.

The cost differential between factoring and invoice discounting

Factoring has benefits it can offer to potential clients, although these are reflected in a higher cost structure than that of invoice discounting. A potential user of the facilities should ask themselves how important non-disclosure is to them.

Most companies prefer an invoice discounting facility, as there is very limited involvement, if any, from the discounter, and the fee structure is less. However, at the smaller level of turnover for ID, the cost differential as compared to factoring is dramatically reduced.

The marketplace can typically support companies turning over £750 000 per annum for ID, providing the financial strength of the client company is present. However, the minimum income clauses imposed to run an ID facility are typically around £6000 per annum, i.e. about 0.7% of gross turnover.

A factoring facility, however, automatically provides the factor with most of the reporting information they require to monitor the performance of their security. The value added of factoring at levels of turnover of up to £1.25m can make it more attractive to factor rather than invoice discount from a purely commercial point of view.

The average factoring client turning over £1m per annum would probably pay 0.9–1% for a recourse factoring facility, which over the year would costs £10.6–11.7k. An ID facility would typically cost 0.6% with a minimum of £6k per annum. The added costs of £4.6–5.7k for the subcontracting of the whole of the credit management and credit control can become highly attractive, competing very favourable with the costs of running an efficient sales ledger in-house.

Hidden charges

As with any newer industry, pricing structures have not been standardised. A number of factors and discounters have a number of hidden charges, which bolster their returns but compromise a client's costs. Amongst the key hidden charges are:

- Arrangement/commitment fees prior to a business being supported. A number of factors request upfront fees of anywhere between £500 and £1500 as a commitment to their undertaking the expense of a 'survey' (i.e. a mini audit) of a company's books. This fee is typically refundable if the factor decides not to support a client's business, although it is vital that a potential user of the facility confirms this at the time of negotiation.
- There are upfront costs incurred when the factoring companies take a client on. The agreed administration fee will be charged against a new client's outstanding sales ledger when the factor first advances cash to them. If a client is paying an administration fee of 1% and their out-standing sales ledger is £200 000, a one-off fee of £2000 will be incurred – effectively representing the factor's arrangement fee.
- The costs of transferring monies – most factors and discounters will transfer monies via BACS without charge, but the costs of Telegraphic Transfer/CHAPS vary markedly throughout the industry between £10 and £50.
- Debits and credits are 'value dated' to a client's account. The number of days of value dating typically varies between two and ten days. Look out especially for the value dating on BACS entries, which will have hit the client's account as a cleared item.
- Some factors charge for credit limit applications.
- Renewal fees may be charged on the anniversary of the agreement, similar in nature to bank review charges.
- There are charges in terminating an agreement. The factors have different notice periods for the termination of a facility. If a client seeks to leave a factor early a termination fee may be levied, equivalent to the factor's lost

income for the notice period. For example a company turning over £1m (gross) and paying 0.9% would expect to have to pay approximately £2250.

- Discounting charges quoted to a client may be charged on a compound basis, as compared to the actual daily balance outstanding at any given time. If charged on a compound basis, the cost of funds negotiated are understated.
- A number of factors and discounters set a minimum percentage below which the cost of funds cannot drop, regardless of the prevailing bank base rate. At the time of writing low interest rates prevail (5.75%), although within a number of factoring agreements the cost of funds are fixed at 10%.
- Some recourse factors charge 'refactoring fees' of between 0.5% and 1.0%. These fees are charged to take into account the additional costs of continuing to chase old invoices (typically over 90 days old).
- If the administration fee includes bad debt protection, what percentage of the debt is covered in the event of customer default? The costs of legal action may be split with a client on a pro-rata basis even if the debt is approved, especially if only 80% cover is offered. Equally, when can payment be expected in the event of debtor insolvency?
- Loss of records insurance – under an invoice discounting facility you may be required to produce proof that if your computerised system failed, that insurance was in place to cover the reinstatement of the lost data which the discounter needs. If you do not have this insurance, the factor may debit your account, at about 0.15–0.2% of the average funds drawn from the discounter.

Source: adapted from the summary checklist of hidden charges published by Cashflow Solutions Ltd.

NOTES

1   Some of the independent factors have an external credit insurance policy where they subcontract to their clients.

Chapter 6

Factoring and invoice discounting versus the bank overdraft

Bank charges for small businesses appear to be on the increase and the factoring market is becoming more competitive – how has this changed their relative costings? In this chapter we help the small business and the financial advisor to compare costs as well as look at the benefits of each of the services. As the criticism of 'cost' is so frequently levelled at the factoring and invoice discounting markets we analyse why so little has been done to counter this criticism by direct comparison with the major source of working capital for UK companies.

COST – AN ISSUE NOT ADDRESSED

Marketing people have succeeded in convincing most business influencers that more working capital can be obtained through factoring than through debtor-linked overdraft. But this is where the effectiveness has stopped. The majority of advisors acknowledge benefits of the facilities but rarely recommend them. Cost is cited frequently as a deterrent to recommending factoring and invoice discounting (Chapter 16).

Why then has the industry not addressed these issues head on? We refer in particular to the main players who are the ones that should be more able, by dint of their size, to influence the business market. Cost comparisons, especially between the bank overdraft and the 'lower priced' product, invoice discounting, do not figure in the marketing campaigns of the bank-owned factors.

As discussed later in the book, we feel that the main reason for this is that they cannot be seen to be directly in competition with one of the major products of the parent bank (bank compliance would not approve any advertising which could be construed as 'negative' to the bank and its services).

The ambivalence of some of the mainstream players is further evidenced by the response we had to a recent enquiry regarding overdraft and invoice discounting costs: The Association of British Factors and Discounters' (ABF&D) information line quoted us typical costs for invoice discounting; a service fee of 0.25% and a discount (finance) charge of 3% over bank base rate. They suggested that typical overdraft rates are 3% above base. No mention was made of arrangement, renewal, management and transaction charges that are part of the overall cost of the overdraft.

They may be happy enough for the moment to bow to the constraint of 'compliance' with the banks' wishes because between 30% and 80% of new business is passed directly to them by the same parent bank. However, should one of the bank-owned factoring companies undergo an MBO or a major new player enter the market, we could look forward to an advertising campaign comparing factoring or invoice discounting and bank lending.

In the absence of any industry guidelines we set out below how companies can assess for themselves which of the services is better value and which is better suited to their business. We look at the benefits often overlooked by those not familiar with the factoring industry, e.g. security, and at 'hidden' costs involved in all three services.

Selection of the most suitable working capital facility, whether it be a bank overdraft, factoring or invoice discounting should be made on the basis of a cost/benefit analysis. The continuing increase in bank lending charges to small businesses which we foresee will make the close scrutiny and comparison of facility costs a regular part of the professional advisor's client care.

Advisors and directors may find the blank tables at the end of the chapter (Tables 6.4 and 6.5) useful for comparing facilities on a case by case basis. Used in conjunction with Figure 6.1 readers can arrive at a true comparison.

We should make the point that the reluctance to confront the issue of cost vis-à-vis the bank overdraft in advertising campaigns is not shared by the direct sales force. Salespeople frequently set out savings and benefits in relation to the overdraft but without the backing of a consistent corporate message this can be construed 'Well, they would say that, wouldn't they?'

HOW PRICE IS MADE UP

A reflection of risk

As we have seen in the previous chapter, cost is directly linked to perceived risk and the perceived ability to manage that risk. Factors and invoice discounters are experts in their field; with the computer systems and staff to assess and manage risks associated with receivables financing. They have the ability to react quickly and 'collect out' their exposure from debtors in the event of a client ceasing to trade. Discounters are generally more successful at 'realising their investment' in the sales ledger than are banks who are lending against receivables.

Bank managers are responsible for 'retailing' around two hundred products and for running around the same number of accounts. There is no way, with the banks organised as they are currently, that each manager can devote a lot of time to monitoring the risk of each loan or advance. Managers typically take a broader view of their customers' business and monitoring of the sales ledger forms only a part of their management of the account. When clients fail, realisation of exposure would be through the receiver or liquidator.

Because factors and invoice discounters – our new commercial bankers – can better manage the risks and secure an exit route the insurance premium element of the facility costs can be kept low. See Table 6.1 for a comparison of bank and factoring solutions to the problems of small businesses.

Table 6.1   Comparison: bank solutions versus factoring solutions

Small business profile	Bank solution	Factoring solution*
Few fixed assets – lack of bank support	Advice not to overtrade	Finance linked to sales around 50–70%
Inexperienced in credit management	Advice to take up references or use a credit checking agency	Credit management provided. Sources, in-house database, on-line information from credit reference agencies and Companies House
Seeking to avoid fixed overheads		Credit control provided
Less able to support credit periods		Finance available on production of approved invoices**
Less able to survive bad debt losses		Bad debt protection option
More likely to deal with high risk customers	Don't trade with poor quality customers	Credit assessments given. Credit limits may be provided

* Factors will not take on all companies, for example those involved in building contracting, and generally those projecting less than £100 000 turnover in their first year.
** Some factors will pay out once a week to small business clients to save on administration.

The raw material – cash

Banks will generally obtain 'cheaper funds' than discounters. The latter will obtain finance from their parent bank or investors for which they will pay a margin.

Overheads

These relate to the people and systems that run the services. As illustrated above factors and invoice discounters have had years of experience in this one aspect of commercial lending. Some were established as long ago as 1960 in the UK. Computer systems have been developed over the years to run ledgers, collections procedures, credit assessment and to automate the gathering of invoice details and the amount of cash advanced. Factors have achieved economies of scale and continue to strive to reduce the number of employees relative to the number of clients. The banks do not have the trained personnel or the systems to manage receivables financing in the same way.

The factors' overheads are necessary to reducing the risks of advancing funds.

QUANTIFYING THE BENEFITS

More cash

To enable the reader to focus on the relative real costs of the services, we have used an example below. For ease of comparison we show the same amount of funds being raised from invoice discounting as from the debtor-linked overdraft, even though discounting will generally provide a lot more cash. We estimate that invoice discounting will generate around 30–70% more funding than the bank overdraft will from the same asset, i.e. the sales ledger.

Bank overdraft finance is typically subject to a gearing ratio of 100% to net assets. As the value of many properties has fallen during the recession the total amount the banks can lend under this formula will be reduced in many cases. Hence the amount of bank funding secured against the sales ledger could diminish further. Conversely any upswing in property values could give security for increased levels of bank funding. It will be interesting to see whether the banks feel as comfortable as they once did with providing finance secured against property.

Calculating the opportunity value of more cash

There are many variables to be taken into account when estimating the amount of extra profit that can be generated by having access to extra funding. Each company works on different margins. Some may find that their working capital needs are totally met by bank finance and that even if more were available it could not be used to win more business. Companies whose funding is limited by a bank manager on the grounds of 'overtrading' should consider the underlying motivation to the manager's recommendation. They may also like to see if the factoring and discounting industry takes the same view and if not, what effect the increased level of working capital would have on the bottom line.

The ability to finance sales is especially vital as the economy recovers. The working capital needed by an average company is around 10% of turnover, given that this amount is usually outstanding to debtors every month. For companies operating on a gross margin of 20% this means that subject to the sales being there, for every extra £1 of working capital available £2 of gross profit can be achieved. Using our example company A below and a gross profit margin of 20% we can see the impact of extra funding:

£10 000 extra working capital finances sales p.a. of   £100 000 = £20 000 gross profit
£300 000   £3 000 000 = £600 000 gross profit

The amount of extra profit which could be generated must be considered when comparing facilities.

Cost/benefit comparison A

Example

Company A: limited company, gross turnover £5 million, average debts outstanding £1 000 000, net worth £500k, 100 customers with outstanding debts at any one time and a gross profit margin of 20%.

Bank overdraft

Low interest charge 3% p.a. above bank base rate (5.75%). Rates will be lower for what the banks see as good customers they wish to retain or where other banking services to the same customer generate a healthy income.

High interest rate 5% p.a. above bank base rate. Interest rates and other related charges will be higher depending on the perceived risk of lending to the particular customer.

Maximum overdraft @ 50% of debtors = £500 000.

Invoice discounting charges

Service charge on discounted turnover 0.25%.

Discount charge on funds drawn down 3% above base rate. Maximum funding line at 80% of debtors and within three times net worth = £800 000 (for cost comparison, £500 000 is used in our example).

You will see from Table 6.2 that when compared to a 'low' priced overdraft the average invoice discounting facility is not much more expensive. However, a highly-priced bank overdraft can be more expensive. In real life, if the discounter perceives the ledger to be a 'good' risk, its funding may be more competitive than the bank's, or the extra costs may be offset by the benefit of flexibility, the additional gross profit that can be generated, no repayment on demand and no personal security being required.

Table 6.2 Comparison: invoice discounting versus the bank overdraft

£500 000 line[1] or overdraft per year	Invoice discounting average (£)	Bank overdraft low (3%) (£)	Bank overdraft high (5%) (£)
Survey fee	500[2]	0	0
Negotiation/arrangement/annual renewal fee	1 250[3]	3 750[4]	7 500[5]
Interest/discount[6]	43 750	43 750	53 750[7]
Processing cheques in./statements	Generally paid by discounter	£600[8]	£732[9]
Management/service fee	12 750[10]	0	1 440[11]
Total	**57 750**	**48 100**	**63 422**

Value added elements			
Opportunity value of extra working capital of £10k	(20 000)[12]		
Fixed interest rate	No	Sometimes	Sometimes
Withdrawal of facility	Notice period given[13]	On demand	On demand
Bad debt protection	Optional extra	No	No
Credit assessment inf.	Yes	No	No
Security	Assignment of debts[14]	Debenture	Debenture
Personal guarantees taken	Rare	Often	Yes
Purchase of insurance, e.g. Keyman, interest rate	Not required	Sometimes required	Sometimes required

[1] In general 30–50% more funding is available from invoice discounting than an overdraft linked to the sales ledger.
[2] Typically refundable on commencement of discounting. Not always charged.
[3] 0.25% service fee levied on outstanding ledger on commencement of facility.
[4] 0.75% of overdraft.
[5] Calculated at 1.5%, the highest we were quoted.
[6] At 3% above bank base rate. For invoice discounting there may be a percentage below which the discount rate will not drop regardless of the bank rate.
[7] Calculated at 5% over base rate currently at 5.75.
[8] Say 100 cheques in per month @ 50p = £50 × 12 months.
[9] Say 100 cheques in per month @ 60p, plus 12 monthly statements @ £1.00.
[10] At 0.25% × £5 million turnover.
[11] Twelve hours of bank manager's time @ £60.
[12] Based on gross profit margin of 20%, costs of extra finance to be deducted.
[13] One to six months.
[14] A charge on debts may be registered.

With competitive pricing in the discounting market – aimed at attracting good quality business – it is possible that overdraft costs can be undercut by discounters. Even small increases in bank charges could mean that invoice discounting is regularly found to be cheaper.

We would suggest to companies looking for working capital finance that they obtain an offer from their bank and from three invoice discounters, from mainstream and smaller operators. We hope we have given the reader the tools with which to assess their relative merits.

No longer 'safe as houses'

Security has become an even more important issue post recession with the eroding of the value of property. As described by one of our interviewees the UK has a 'bricks and mortar' economy. Lending has traditionally been secured by company or directors' personal real estate.

As we go into recovery and property values do not appear to be increasing to pre-recession levels many more companies will find that their biggest asset is the debtor book or sales ledger. Companies will need to make the best use of this asset in terms of raising adequate working capital. Banks will want to continue to lend to protect income streams and cross-sell other services but the amount of finance made available to the small business sector is likely to be less than it was in the 1980s.

The security for lending required by the banks is typically a fixed and floating charge on all the company's assets and directors' personal guarantees. That generally required by invoice discounters and factors is an assignment of the book debts and in some cases a charge in the form of a debenture and/or directors' personal guarantees. The advantage to the company is that other assets, property, equipment, etc. are generally left unencumbered and can be subject to other, more appropriate financing tools, for example medium-term loans and leasing.

Immediate withdrawal versus notice period

Over the last three or four years the banks have not only been criticised for causing the failure of many small companies by not granting or withdrawing funding overnight but also for the dramatic effect their actions have had on the lives of individuals. We have seen stories of the family home being sold by the bank to repay directors' business commitments and the break-up of marriages and families.

Many feel that business is risky enough without having to chance one's family and home. Entrepreneurs may feel more strongly than ever that using personal assets to secure a business loan is to be avoided thus giving them another reason to view factoring and invoice discounting positively.

The effects of the ability of the banks to withdraw funding, more or less immediately, have also been made graphically clear in the media. The factors' and discounters' closer contact with the sales activities of their clients make withdrawal of facilities less likely and anyway termination periods can be anything up to one year.

CROSS SELLING BY BANKS INCREASES REAL COSTS

Directors may not take kindly to various insurances being required by the bank to enable the sanctioning of an overdraft. Mark Spofforth, Vice-Chairman of the Institute of Chartered Accountants' General Practitioners Board told us:

If someone goes in [to the bank] to negotiate an overdraft, negotiations suddenly become dependent upon keyman insurance, insurance against interest rates increasing ... and although these things are very rarely written down there is no doubt that a level of blackmail has been used by bank managers to sell these products on top of overdraft facilities. The customer feels that the bank manager has been a salesman.

Flexibility

The case for factoring and invoice discounting is summed up by Paul Samrah of chartered accountants, Kingston Smith: 'Invoice discounting and factoring are infinitely more flexible than a bank overdraft – the bank overdraft is usually payable on demand and is of course subject to a fixed limit.' Some bank managers we have interviewed dispute this, saying that the overdraft is not subject to credit limits on individual customers and disputed debts are still financed. These are valid points but as a whole factoring and invoice discounting will generate substantially more working capital against the sales ledger out-weighing these considerations. It is worth noting too that some factors do not issue credit limits per debtor.

   If a company needs to increase an overdraft to cover a large new order it will need to renegotiate the facility. This can take time and money putting a proposal to the bank manager (whose time you may be paying for too) and gaining approval. Approval is by no means certain. The factoring facility requires no such renegotiation. Both factors and discounters are very much in tune with the sales function of their client – increases in clients' sales means an increase in income for the factor. Banks generally link lending to a company's total assets – bank managers have more to consider when agreeing extra funding. Temporary increases to the discounting line to cover exceptional orders can often be easily agreed.

FACTORING – ADDED VALUE OR UNNECESSARY EXTRA?

The factoring service fee covers the expenses involved in running the client's sales ledger. So that this does not become an extra perceived cost to the client, staff engaged in the credit management function may need to be deployed elsewhere. Often the sales ledger clerk takes on other duties as well as liaising with the factor and monitoring their effectiveness. Companies using factoring can avoid the fixed overhead of employing administrative staff without being certain of work levels. The sub-contracting to external suppliers of non-core business activities will no doubt spread, giving a boost to the factors. Disregarding for a moment the finance aspects of the facility, factoring sales ledger administration could be justified as part of the general trend away from fixed overheads to variable overheads. Removing some of the burden of fixed overheads from small firms makes good business sense.

THE COST OF FACTORING

The service element being greater in factoring than in invoice discounting there are extra areas of benefit for the potential user to consider rather than simply comparing charges with those of the overdraft. These fall under two headings of potential savings, debt chasing and credit management plus the benefit of freeing directors/managers' time from work that can be done more effectively and cheaply by others. These are in addition to the opportunity value of extra funding being available in most cases and the lesser requirement for security, as described for invoice discounting above.

To help the reader assess the value to their firm, we have put the service elements under the subheadings listed in Figure 6.1. To compare costs with the overdraft we are using the example of company A, with a factoring prepayment of £500 000. Around £200 000 more than this would usually be available against outstandings of £1 million but for ease of illustration we have reduced this to the maximum amount available from an overdraft against the same ledger. The factoring fee is estimated at 0.9% of turnover and includes bad debt protection, i.e. is a non-recourse facility.

Table 6.3 shows that the cost justification for using factoring relies on two value added elements – the savings to be made and the opportunity value of having more cash to make more profits. That is why it is so important to assess each function that can be taken over by the factor and what a company stands to gain from having access to more working capital.

POINTS TO REMEMBER

When comparing invoice discounting and factoring with the bank overdraft here are some points to remember:

- Obtain offers in principle and endeavour to compare 'like for like'.
- If the bank will not offer finance (possibly due to lack of security and therefore perceived high risk) but the factor will, you should not attempt to compare the factoring charges with hypothetical bank charges.
- Around 30–70% more cash can in general be generated from the sales ledger asset by using factoring or invoice discounting (compared to the bank overdraft). The 'opportunity' value of the extra cash should be included in your comparison.
- Banks normally provide between 30% and 50% against debtors but this is generally subject to an overall gearing ratio of 100%. Invoice discounting will provide up to 80% against debtors, with the gearing ratio of around 250–300%. Gearing is not used to calculate funding for a factoring facility.
- Bank overdrafts are repayable on demand. Changes in a company's circumstances could lead on to a potentially disastrous withdrawal of funding. Factoring and invoice discounting provide a notice period within the agreement, ranging from one to six months.

Table 6.3   Comparison: full service factoring versus the bank overdraft

£500 000 line[1] or overdraft per year	Full service factoring average (£)	Bank overdraft low (3%)(£)	Bank overdraft high (5%) (£)
Survey fee	500[2]	0	0
Negotiation/arrangement/annual renewal fee	9 000[3]	3 750[4]	7.500[5]
Interest/discount[6]	43 750	43 750	53 750[7]
Management/service fee	45 000[8]	0	1 440[9]
Total	**97 750**	**47 500**	**62 690**
Potential savings			
Chasing payments	(15 000)	N/A	N/A
Credit checking/assessment	(15 000)	N/A	N/A
Bad debt protection	(5 000)	N/A	N/A
Tel., fax, postage, etc.	(1 000)	N/A	N/A
Prompt payment discount	(5 000)	N/A	N/A
Opportunity value of extra working capital per £10k	(20 000)	Not available	Not available
Total potential savings	**(61 000)**	**None**	**None**
Costs less savings	**36 750**	**47 500**	**62 690**
Fixed interest rate	No	Sometimes	Sometimes
Withdrawal of facility	Notice period given[10]	On demand	On demand
Security	Assignment of debts[11]	Debenture	Debenture
Personal guarantees taken	Rare	Often	Yes
Purchase of Insurance, e.g. Keyman, interest rate	Not required	Sometimes required	Sometimes required

[1] In general 30–50% more funding is available from factoring than an overdraft linked to the sales ledger.
[2] Typically refundable on commencement of discounting. Not always charged.
[3] 0.9% service fee levied on outstanding ledger on commencement of facility.
[4] 0.75% of overdraft.
[5] Calculated at 1.5%, the highest we were quoted.
[6] At 3% above bank base rate.
[7] Calculated at 5% over base rate currently at 5.75.
[8] At 0.9% × £5 million turnover.
[9] Twelve hours of bank manager's time @ £60.
[10] One to six months.
[11] A charge on debts may be registered.

The potential savings and opportunities guide
Chasing payments
Appointing staff to carry out this function £
Directors' time chasing overdue payments @ £   per hour
Staff time chasing overdue payments @ £   per hour
Time instructing a solicitor to collect outstandings @ £ per hour
Legal costs associated with collecting
Phone, fax and postage
Sending statements
Improvement in debtor days outstanding (generally a minimum of 10%) and the subsequent reduction in interest charges on borrowings

Credit checking
Appointing/training staff to carry out this function
Time involved in checking creditworthiness of new customers @ £   per hour
Costs of obtaining bank and credit agency references @ £   per hour
Staff time spent analysing the references and allocating a credit limit @ £   per hour
Costs of credit insurance if any
Losses due to bad debts

Better use of directors' time
What are the following worth to your company?
More cash to pay suppliers and obtain prompt payment discounts, 1–2%
More free time to devote to running the business and developing more sales, rather than chasing payment for sales already made

Total per annum £

Figure 6.1   The potential savings and opportunities guide

MAKING YOUR EXIT FROM INVOICE DISCOUNTING AND FACTORING

Another major criticism of factoring and invoice discounting is that 'once you are in, it's difficult to get out'.

Aubrey Selig, Vice-Chairman of the Association of Invoice Factors, summarises this situation for us: 'If you have any financial service, be it a bank loan, hire purchase, leasing, factoring or invoice discounting the Agreement provides for termination ... A problem can arise where the client wants to terminate the Agreement but has no positive plan to repay the factor. Then, the only course is to wind down the agreement by phasing the repayment to the factor...'

Terminating a factoring or invoice discounting facility, a bank loan or overdraft requires repayment of the funds advanced. This is not so much a difficulty as a clear practicality.

The real difficulty with ending the agreement arises where some factors or discounters require an unduly long notice period or payment of termination charges in lieu. Many allow three months or less, and at the time of writing Kellock Limited are offering immediate termination with no penalty.

INDUSTRY CHANGE IS NEEDED

Three months is, in our view, a reasonable time but we would prefer the industry as a whole to respond to criticism and reduce the notice periods required of clients, to a maximum of one month, notifiable at any time. On the other hand, where the factor wishes to terminate an agreement, we suggest a longer period – say three months – should be standardised to allow the client to find other sources of funding. Overdrafts can be repaid at any time and here is one clear instance where it wins out over factoring.

LONG NOTICE PERIODS – SOME JUSTIFICATION

Some factors currently insist on a period of six months or more and others only allow notification to be given on the anniversary of the agreement. One reason for imposing notice periods or termination fees is that factors and invoice discounters do not generally start making a profit from their clients until nine months or a year into the operation of the facility.

There is some justification for a longer termination period where, for example, a factor or invoice discounter has agreed a particularly low discount rate, say base rate for the first six months of the facility followed by a capped rate for the following half year. In this case penalty payments can be likened to early repayment charges associated with a fixed rate bank loan.

Potential factoring clients and their advisors should check the wording of the proposed agreement for conditions of termination before signing.

NEGOTIATE

Those who wish to terminate their agreement and have a repayment plan, as mentioned by Selig above, are in a relatively strong negotiating position. Although factors and invoice discounters give the conditions of termination in their agreements, clients may be able to negotiate better terms – it is the case that factors and discounters do not want to retain a vociferous, unhappy client.

DISSATISFACTION

Transferring to another factor/invoice discounter or extending bank facilities will be no problem if the client's business is of sufficient quality. Any reasonable causes of dissatisfaction with the current factor should be notified to the relevant representative body: the Association of Invoice Factors, the Association of British Factors & Discounters or the Commercial Finance Association.

WINDING DOWN THE FACILITY

This is usually done during the notice period or other agreed term. The level of funding is gradually reduced by the factor/discounter so that at the end of the period no funding is outstanding to the client, e.g. Jones & Co. Ltd, at the time of giving notice, receive 75% funding against approved invoices, the notice period is three months, both parties agree a reduction in financing of 25% per month.

Where there is no replacement funding, clients should be wary of potential liquidity problems.

Summary

Comparing invoice discounting with the overdraft is a fairly straightforward exercise and the relative pricing should be competitive. However, few businesspeople and their advisors seriously consider discounting as an alternative to overdraft finance. For many companies discounting can offer greater flexibility in terms of the amount of cash made available and its ability to meet peaks in demand for working capital.

The total package of benefits that factoring can bring needs to be understood when comparing costs with those of the overdraft. The added-value elements and potential savings must be costed to compare fairly. Opting for or dismissing factoring on the grounds of expense should only be done after a detailed cost/benefit analysis.

Table 6.4 Blank table: invoice discounting versus the bank overdraft

£500 000 line or overdraft per year	Invoice discounting average (£)	Bank overdraft low (3%) (£)	Bank overdraft high (5%) (£)
Survey fee			
Negotiation/arrangement/annual renewal fee			
Interest/discount			
Processing cheques in./statements			
Management/service fee			
Total			
Value added elements			
Opportunity value of extra working capital of £10k			
Fixed interest rate			
Withdrawal of facility			
Bad debt protection			
Credit assessment inf.			
Security			
Personal guarantees taken			
Purchase of insurance, e.g. Keyman, interest rate			

Table 6.5 Blank table: full service factoring versus the bank overdraft

£500 000 line or overdraft per year	Full service factoring average (£)	Bank overdraft low (3%) (£)	Bank overdraft high (5%) (£)
Survey fee			
Negotiation/arrangement/annual renewal fee			
Interest/discount			
Management/service fee			
Total			
Potential savings			
Chasing payments			
Credit checking/assessment			
Bad debt protection			
Tel., fax, postage, etc.			
Prompt payment discount			
Opportunity value of extra working capital per £10k			
Total potential savings **Costs less savings**			
Fixed interest rate			
Withdrawal of facility			
Security			
Personal guarantees taken			
Purchase of Insurance, e.g. Keyman, interest rate			

Chapter 7

Marketing versus reality: how much finance will factoring actually generate?

The factoring industry as a whole has sought to break away from the 'last resort finance' stigma which has historically blocked its emergence as the up and coming financing tool. To this end, factoring facilities are heavily marketed, selling the key benefits of flexibility and the ability to generate increased funds as compared to the overdraft. But how does the marketing actually compare with the reality – how much finance will actually be generated?

The factoring industry markets its services as providing up to 85% finance against approved invoices. It is the vagaries of 'up to' and 'approved', which determine the actual level of finance generated from a company's given sales ledger using a factoring facility.

As we have seen in Chapter 4, the factor will always seek to have a margin, i.e. the unfinanced portion of the invoices. If an 80% facility is offered, the factor automatically has a margin of 20%. This margin affords the factor protection against the problems of collecting monies from an insolvent client's customers. The greater the perceived risks the greater the margin they require.

In reality, the majority of factoring companies actually generate substantially less than the 80% or 85% indicated within the marketing literature. It is the 'approved' invoices which are financed by the factor. So what influences the factor's decision to 'approve' an invoice?

RETENTIONS

Besides the safety margin required by the factor, monies will be held back from their client's sales ledger for a variety of reasons, called 'retentions' or reserves.

As seen in Chapter 4, anything that can stop the customer paying an invoice will compromise the factor's ability to recoup their funds in a terminal situation. Anything that will compromise this ability to obtain payment will be unapproved, will be held by the factor as a retention and will remain unfinanced.

Additionally, it is important to recognise that unlike fixed-asset finance, a factor's security changes every day. As the profile of the security changes, so does the level of finance generated.

There are four key retentions that will restrict the level of funds advanced by the factor:

- disputed debts
- credit unapproved debts
- spread of debts
- old debts.

1. Disputes

The factor deals in paper, the clients in goods and services. As a result, the factor has no control over the quality of the goods or services offered, all they can do is react to the facts before them. In the course of chasing the outstanding invoices for payment, the factor will naturally come across customers who are not satisfied with the goods or services received. At the time a factor is notified by the client's customer of a dispute, they cannot collect the outstanding debt, and will therefore withdraw funding against those invoices that are disputed.

Whether spurious or otherwise, the factor will withhold payment from any disputed invoices as a control mechanism, until such time as the dispute has been resolved to the customer's satisfaction. With there being a clear financial incentive for the client, disputes tend to be resolved quickly.

The factor notifies their client of their intentions via a 'dispute notice' or 'query memo', which is sent to the client detailing the nature of the dispute as indicated by the customer, as soon as a dispute is notified (Figure 7.1).

Within the dispute notice, the reason for non-payment by the client's customer is detailed. As can be seen, certain classification of dispute will render the invoice concerned unapproved from a funding point of view.

There is usually a fixed time period, approximately 28 days, by which time the dispute needs to be resolved, failing which the invoice will be 'reassigned' to the client. In other words, if the dispute remains unresolved, the factor will relinquish all responsibility for collecting that debt, passing the responsibility back to the client company, and withdrawing any finance advanced against it.

2. Credit unapproved debts

The standard control mechanism for any business, the customer credit limit, is so often flouted in the face of external commercial pressures. However,

Metropolitan Factors Limited

CLIENT:	No:
CUSTOMER:	No:

DISPUTE NOTICE

No: 01766

Date:

We are advised by your customer that payment of the undermentioned invoice/s is not being made for the reason indicated.

If the customer is correct, please raise and forward to us a credit note at once; otherwise please advise the steps you have taken to adjust the dispute by completing and returning to us the duplicate copy of this notice.

	* INVOICE NO.	DATE	AMOUNT
1			
2			
3			
4			
5			
6			
*	Denotes status change to unapproved		

☐ Paid direct
☐ Not delivered
☐ Price Query
☐ Wrong Quantity
☐ Faulty
☐ Goods Returned
☐ Not Ordered
☐ Late Delivery
☐ POD Required

OTHER COMMENTS

SIGNED: . . . .

ANSWER BY CLIENT:-

SIGNED . . . .   DATE:. . . . .

ORIGINAL TO BE RETURNED TO MFL
COPY TO BE RETAINED BY CLIENT

1212190006

Figure 7.1 Dispute notice (reproduced courtesy of Metropolitan Factors Limited)

exceeding the limits set by the credit manager may have implications for bad debts. Factors react in the same way.

The majority set credit limits on their client's customers, with the limits individually judged against the cold credit assessment of the latter's credit-worthiness. These credit limits can also act as 'financing limits'.

Should the client choose to trade with a given customer beyond this set credit limit, the factor under its agreement with the client is not under any obligation to finance the invoice value beyond the limit set. They will 'unap-prove' any invoices factored over the credit limit and not finance the unap-proved portion. It should be noted, however, that a number of factors take a commercial view of the 'credit unapproved' invoices and choose to finance a portion of the unapproved debts, although they may seek to charge the client for this flexibility.

3. Spread of debts

Factoring companies rely upon their risks being diversified. To this end, they generally do not wish to see a major customer forming more than 25–30% of the outstanding sales ledger. Any invoices raised to the major customer, which exceed the spread threshold set by the factor, will not be financed.

4. Disapproval for age

With recourse factors, i.e. where credit protection is not offered, the factor will seek to render any old invoices as 'unapproved'. Typically, if credit control has been undertaken effectively, old debts will have underlying problems associated with them – either they are disputed or the customers may be experiencing financial difficulties. Most recourse factors will withhold pay-ment from invoices that are 90 days past the due date. Some, however, may withhold funds when invoices are 60 days past the due date.

THE CHANGING FINANCING LEVELS FOR THOSE USING A FACTORING FACILITY

(For the sake of clarity and ease of use, the factor's charges are not taken into consideration in evaluationg the availability of funds.) The level of retentions detailed above will directly restrict the level of finance advanced to a given company. Consider the example of a manufacturing company, XYZ Ltd turning over £2m, which uses a recourse factor to factor its debts. The factor is assumed to collect its client's debts in approximately 71 days.

Turnover (gross)	£2m
Outstanding invoices	£392k

Table 7.1 Sample invoice ages for XYZ LTD

Total Outstanding	Current	30 days	60 days	90 days	Over 90 days
£392k	£190k	£110k	£45k	£35K	£12k
	48.5%	28%	11.5%	8.9%	3.1%

Assume the invoices age as in Table 7.1. Assume that after assessing the creditworthiness of the customers, 5% of the outstanding invoices, i.e. £20k, are either not approved or exceed the credit limits set by the factor. Finally assume the average level of trading disputes is 2.5% of sales, i.e. £ 10k. The total debts that are unapproved, and therefore unavailable for finance are detailed in Table 7.2.

Table 7.2 Total disapproved debts (i.e. retentions) for XYZ Ltd

Credit unapproved debts	£20k
Disapproval for age	£12k
Disputed debts	£10k
Total disapproved debts for XYZ Ltd	£42k

Total debts outstanding	=	£392k	❶		
Less the following 'reserves /retentions'					
Over 90 days		£12k			
Unapproved debts		£20k			
Disputes		£10k			
Sub-total		£ 42k	❷		
The level of approved debts ❶ – ❷	=	£392k – £42k.	=	£350k	❸
Total available funding at 80% of approved debts (i.e. ❸ × 80%)	=	£280k	❹		
Thus the **actual** percentage advanced against the outstanding sales ledger (i.e. ❹/❶)	=	71.4%			

Figure 7.2 XYZ Ltd

Consider the funding profile of XYZ Ltd (Figure 7.2) assuming the factor advances 80% of approved debts. Thus although the factor may market that they will advance up to 80% of approved invoices, the reality is that just over 70% is available for the client company. It is not untypical for a factor to advance a net figure of around 65–70% after retentions are taken into consideration. Indeed this net figure can be even less according to the profile of the client's sales ledger.

In evaluating subsequent funds made available to a client company, we need to consider how changes in the profile of the sales ledger will influence the level of finance made available to the client. Generally speaking additional invoices will provide additional finance to the client, as will any payments received from their customers. Suppose XYZ draws all available funds down from the factor in example one:

Total available funds   £280k
Total funds drawn by the client £280k

Total debts outstanding (brought forward)		=	£392k			
New approved invoices raised		=	£ 30k			
Total debts outstanding (carried forward)		=	£422k		❶	
Less the existing 'reserves /retentions'						
Over 90 days		£12k				
Unapproved debts		£20k				
Disputes		£10k				
		———				
Sub-total		£ 42k			❷	
		———				
The level of approved debts ❶ – ❷	=	£422k – £42k	=	£380k	❸	
Total available funding at 80% of	=	£304k	❸ (72%)			
approved debts (i.e ❸ × 80%)						
Funds already drawn (client's current account)	=	£280k	❺			
Available funds (i.e.❹ – ❺)	=	£24k	(i.e. 80% of new invoices)			
Funds drawn	=	£24k				
Total funds drawn	=	£304k				

Figure 7.3   XYZ Ltd – submission of new approved invoices, £30k

Suppose £30k of gross invoices are now factored, all of which are credit approved. The results are shown in Figure 7.3. Now suppose two approved customers pay £30k for outstanding debts, which were thirty days old (Figure 7.4). These examples, which show how the client's sales ledger profile will change daily, can have serious implications for a client in planning their own cash flow. Consider the final example of XYZ Ltd, who find that:

● one of their customers disputes £8k of work;
● their major customer files weak accounts at Companies House, with that customer's credit limit reviewed downwards by £20k.

The disapproved debts for XYZ Ltd will change accordingly (Table 7.3).

Table 7.3   Disapproved debts for XYZ Ltd

	From (£)	To (£)
Credit unapproved debts	20k	40k
Disapproval for age	12k	12k
Disputed debts	10k	18k
Total disapproved debts	42k	70k

Total debts outstanding (brought forward)	=	£422k	❶	
Cash paid	=	£30k	❻	
New debts outstanding	=	£392k		
Less the existing 'reserves /retentions'				
Over 90 days		£12k		
Unapproved debts		£20k		
Disputes		£10k		
Sub-total		£ 42k	❷	
The level of approved debts ❶ – ❷	=	£392k – £42k.	=	£350k ❸
Total available funding at 80% of approved debts (i.e ❸ × 80%)	=	£280k	❹ (71.4%)	
Factor's account (brought forward)	=	£304k	❺	
Cash received from customer	=	£ 30k	❻	
Factor's account (carried forward)	=	£274k	❼ (❺ – ❻)	
Available funds (i.e. ❹ – ❼) (i.e. 20% of customer payment)	=	£6k	❽	

Figure 7.4   XYZ Ltd – £30k cash received from approved customers

Total debts outstanding (carried forward)	=	£392k	❶	
Less the following 'reserves/retentions'				
Over 90 days		£12k		
Unapproved debts		£40k		
Disputes		£18k		
Sub-total		£ 70k	❷	
The level of approved debts ❶ – ❷	=	£392k – £70k.	=	£322k ❸
Funding at 80% of approved debts (i.e. ❸ × 80%)	=	£258k	❹	
Funds already taken (from Figure 7.3)	=	£274k		
Factor's **overexposure**	=	£16k		
Thus the **actual** percentage advanced against the outstanding sales ledger (i.e. ❹/❶)	=	65.7%		

Figure 7.5   XYZ Ltd – change in profile of the sales ledger

The funding profile of XYZ Ltd changes accordingly, as shown in Figure 7.5. The client company had already drawn £274k of funds from the factoring company. The available funds, however, stood at £258k, leaving the factor over-exposed or 'overdrawn' by £16k. No additional finance will now be provided by the factor until new invoices or cash receipts from the client's customers have been received, which will remove the overdrawn position.

As the profile of the client's debtor book changes, so the factor's security will change. As a result, it can sometimes be very difficult for the client to plan their cash flow effectively. Table 7.4 highlights the features that will affect the availability of funds from a factor to a client company.

Table 7.4 Summary of features affecting a factoring client's availability of finance

Feature	Increase in available funds	Decrease in available funds
Disputes notified by customer		✓
Customer credit unapproved		✓
Issuance of credit notes		✓
Contra taken by customer		✓
Settlement discount		✓
Debts ageing beyond 90 days		✓
Exceeding the 'spread' threshold		✓
Factoring/discount charges		✓
Raising invoices	✓	
Payment by customer	✓	
Resolution of dispute	✓	
Increased credit limit on previously unapproved customer	✓	

PRACTICAL EXAMPLE OF FACTORING FUNDING

Figure 7.6 has been taken from the computers of Metropolitan Factors Ltd using the software of the specialist software development house, Hyams Systems Services Group Ltd. The example shows the 'availability screen' of a given client, which has a prepayment facility of 80% of eligible debts. The principal points to notice from the screen printout are:

- The total security available to the factor, i.e. outstanding invoices = £420 534.
- The approved balance of £407 491 represents the level of debts which are approved for funding purposes.
- Unapproved balances, where the client company has exceeded their credit limits = £6618. These remain unfunded.
- Ineligible debts of £5910, which are debts unapproved for age.
- Disputed debts, £514 are unfunded

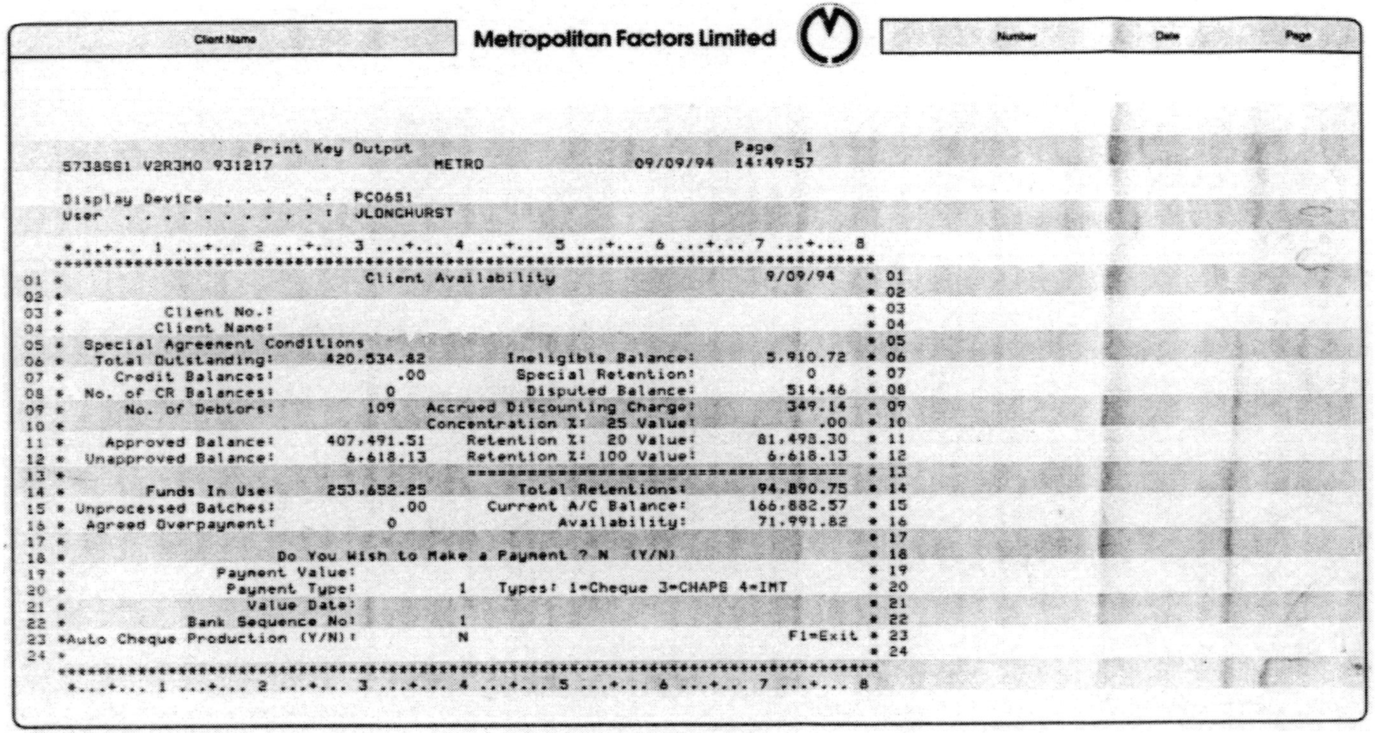

Client Name | Metropolitan Factors Limited | Number | Date | Page

```
                    Print Key Output                                  Page    1
5738SS1 V2R3M0 931217               METRO                  09/09/94  14:49:57

Display Device . . . . . . :  PC06S1
User . . . . . . . . . . . :  JLONCHURST

 *...+... 1 ...+... 2 ...+... 3 ...+... 4 ...+... 5 ...+... 6 ...+... 7 ...+... 8
 *********************************************************************************
01 *                           Client Availability                    9/09/94    * 01
02 *                                                                             * 02
03 *          Client No.:                                                        * 03
04 *         Client Name:                                                       * 04
05 *  Special Agreement Conditions                                               * 05
06 *    Total Outstanding:        420,534.82        Ineligible Balance:  5,910.72 * 06
07 *      Credit Balances:               .00         Special Retention:         0 * 07
08 *  No. of CR Balances:              0             Disputed Balance:    514.46 * 08
09 *      No. of Debtors:            109  Accrued Discounting Charge:    349.14 * 09
10 *                                     Concentration %:  25 Value:       .00 * 10
11 *    Approved Balance:        407,491.51     Retention %:  20 Value: 81,498.30 * 11
12 *  Unapproved Balance:          6,618.13     Retention %: 100 Value:  6,618.13 * 12
13 *                                         ==================================== * 13
14 *        Funds In Use:        253,652.25          Total Retentions: 94,890.75 * 14
15 * Unprocessed Batches:               .00       Current A/C Balance: 166,882.57 * 15
16 *  Agreed Overpayment:              0                 Availability: 71,991.82 * 16
17 *                                                                             * 17
18 *                 Do You Wish to Make a Payment ? N  (Y/N)                    * 18
19 *              Payment Value:                                                 * 19
20 *               Payment Type:        1   Types: 1=Cheque 3=CHAPS 4=IMT        * 20
21 *                 Value Date:                                                 * 21
22 *           Bank Sequence No:        1                                        * 22
23 *Auto Cheque Production (Y/N):       N                               F1=Exit * 23
24 *                                                                             * 24
 *********************************************************************************
 *...+... 1 ...+... 2 ...+... 3 ...+... 4 ...+... 5 ...+... 6 ...+... 7 ...+... 8
```

Figure 7.6 Availability screen (reproduced courtesy of Metropolitan Factors Limited)

Metropolitan Factors Limited

Client Name		Number	Date	Page

INELIGIBLE REPORT

09 SEP 94

	DUE DATE	ITEM DATE	VALUE	
SOLICITORS ACCOUNT	UNAPPROVED		3,440.18	INELIGIBLE	4,540.18

CHO2004

	DUE DATE	ITEM DATE	VALUE	
INV NO. 3837	31/01/94	10/12/93	1,377.04	INELIGIBLE
INV NO. 18030001	15/03/94	15/03/94	500.00CR	
INV NO. 3997	31/03/94	18/02/94	3,163.14	INELIGIBLE
On Account Payment	31/07/94	2/06/94	400.00CR	

GA71000

	UNAPPROVED		INELIGIBLE	
INV NO. 4185	31/05/94	29/04/94	1,239.92	1,239.92	INELIGIBLE

ME70000

	UNAPPROVED		INELIGIBLE	
INV NO. 4224	30/06/94	10/05/94	1,030.62	1,030.62	INELIGIBLE

Figure 7.7 Ineligible report (reproduced courtesy of Metropolitan Factors Limited)

Client Name Number Date Page

Metropolitan Factors Limited

UNAPPROVED REPORT FOR CLIENT

AS OF 9/09/94

DEBTOR	DEBTOR NAME	LIMIT	TOTAL O/S	UNAPPROVED	DISPUTED	SOLICITOR
CHA0004		0	3,640.18	3640.18		Solicitors Account
MIL3009		41,000	44,254.95	3254.95		
PL28000		23,000	26,363.18	3363.18		
TOTALS T		TOTAL O/S 420,534.82	UNAPPROVED 19,258.31	DISPUTED 514.46		

Figure 7.8 Unapproved report (reproduced courtesy of Metropolitan Factors Limited)

- Total outstanding   £420 534
    - less unapproved debts   £6618
    - less ineligible debts   £5910
    - less disputed debts   £514
  - generates approved debts, i.e.   £407 491   (which are funded).
- The funds taken by the client are represented by the 'funds in use' figure of £253.6k.
- The client has available funds of £71.9k upon which to draw if required.
- Adding the funds in use to the availability generates the total level of funds that could be drawn from the factor. In this example the maximum funds the client could draw would be £253.6k + £71.9k = £325.5k, which represents 77% of the total security available.
- The total retentions include the automatic 'margin' retention of 20%, i.e. £81.5k.

This is a typical screen the account managers from the various factoring companies will see when assessing the funds that can be released to a given client. Typically, summary reports are sent to a factor's clients to detail the invoices which are unapproved from a funding point of view (Figures 7.7 and 7.8).

Summary

Thus it can be seen that whilst the marketeers detail that finance is available up to 85% of approved invoices, the factors will be in charge of how invoices are approved, with the reality that they will be advancing closer to 65–70% of invoice values. Equally, this value fluctuates daily in accordance with the profile of the client's sales ledger, rendering cash flow planning difficult.

Chapter 8

How to make the most of the facility

While many companies may have been factoring for 10–15 years, the typical factoring and invoice discounting client stays within the industry for between three and five years. The facility enables them to grow effectively enough to establish themselves fully within their own marketplaces and to develop their balance sheet sufficiently to become 'bankable', i.e. their balance sheets become strong enough to support traditional bank borrowings.

So many small businesses, however, take the decision to use factoring and invoice discounting because they are experiencing short-term cash flow difficulties, typically on the way up – through undercapitalisation – rather than on the way down. Their decision can often therefore be made to satisfy short-term objectives rather than medium-term objectives – the reactive decision of solving the short-term financing problem.

The facilities that are available within the marketplace vary markedly, so much so that two factors looking at the same sales ledger and the same company can have two completely separate views regarding the level of financing.

Case study

A reprographic house based in London began trading in January 1992. The managing director had been a shareholding director of his previous employer who was factoring using a mainstream factor, so it was a natural choice to use the same factor for his newly founded business. The factor chosen was a mainstream non-recourse factoring company and a subsidiary of their bankers, who agreed to support the business with residual overdraft facilities.

The client company was a classic case of a new start business seeking to generate business quickly to cover the developing overhead base. At the time of the initial period of business development, the recession was badly affecting many sectors in general and the advertising sector in particular, which formed the key market sector for the client.

The client's debtor book was well spread, with the major customer comprising about 25% of the outstanding sales ledger. The quality of the customers from a credit point of view were only fair, although there was a more positive shift in the quality of customers developing as the client generated quality, high profile results. The factor was setting credit limits and finance limits simultaneously and was not able to provide the credit limits the client required. The debts, however, were being paid in about 75 days.

With the factor limiting the level of finance directly to the credit limits set on the customers, the client was generating only 33% finance against their total debtor book. This was squeezing their cash flow dramatically and arrears were building up with many of their creditors.

A commercial recourse factor was introduced to them. The factor did not set any credit limits on the customers, rather looking at the spread of the customer base and the age of the invoices outstanding. Examining exactly the same sales ledger and exactly the same financial position they were immediately able to refinance the business at 65% of the outstanding sales ledger, almost double the amount being provided by the mainstream factor.

MAXIMISING CASH FLOW

The lessons to be drawn from the case study are that no two factors are the same – each can have a different view of the same client company. In an ideal world, to maximise cash flow from the facility, the sales ledger presented to the factor needs to be 'clean'. All customers would be blue chip, the major customer would represent only 10% of the outstanding sales ledger, the client's products would be very simple in their nature and the client would be highly profitable. Commercial reality determines otherwise.

As we have seen in Chapter 7, the cash flow available from a standard facility will not typically match up to the marketing hype. Cash flow can and does vary from day to day according to the profile of the client company's sales ledger, rendering the 85% funding hype down to a more realistic 65–70%, with the level of finance reduced by the 'retentions' held by a factor:

- disputed debts
- credit unapproved debts
- spread of debts
- old debts.

In order to maximise the level of cash flow available from a facility, it is crucial to adopt a proactive approach to sourcing a factor whose operational style minimises these retentions.

Disputed debts

In all forms of factoring, disputed debts will not be financed. Being uncollec-table at that moment the debt has no value to the factor. Disputed invoices will not be financed until the disputes are resolved, so it is in a client's interest to resolve them quickly. One of the benefits of the on-line computer facilities offered by the factors is that up-to-date information is made available to a client as it happens – this is critical when it comes to notification of disputes. Your cash flow can be severely restricted if your major customer disputes their outstanding invoices, so it is in your interests to know as soon as possible if an invoice is disputed.

Tips and traps – disputed debts

Tips

- When negotiating with the factor, find out how they notify you of disputes and above what invoice level they will automatically telephone you to notify you of the dispute.
- Ensure full paperwork is made available to the factor as soon as a dispute is highlighted.
- Answer the factor's dispute notice/query memo as quickly as possible – this will speed up your funding.

Traps

- Non-recourse factors can seek to remove a credit limit on a disputed debt, rendering the bad debt protection invalid. Equally, the limit may not be reinstated after the dispute has been cleared up.
- If the dispute notice remains unanswered, the debt will be reassigned back to you, in other words the factor will relinquish any further responsibility for collection of the outstanding debt.

Credit unapproved debts

The majority of mainstream facilities will assess their clients' customers and set credit limits against them. These credit limits will also determine the level of funding made available.

The non-recourse factor provides credit protection against approved bad debts. As a result, they are liable for any bad debts incurred by their client on credit approved customers. Given that the factor will suffer financially should a client's customer fail, they will take a closer interest in the creditworthiness of the customer, as it is in their interests to do so. As a result, increased information will be assessed to get a closer reflection of that customer's creditworthiness.

Whilst clearly recognising the benefit of giving their clients clear guidance as to whether it should be safe to undertake business with this customer, it will also have the effect of potentially restricting the likely level of finance provided against that customer. In traditional non-recourse factoring, the credit limit offered by the factor will also reflect the maximum limit to which the factor will advance finance against that customer. Thus the more the information sourced on a customer, the more likely that the credit limit will be more conservatively approached, the less funding would be made available.

Furthermore, if the client decides to ship goods to the value beyond their given credit limit, the non-recourse factor has the right under their agreement to refuse to provide finance against a customer over and beyond their given credit limit. The factor will not say to a client that they cannot trade with a customer beyond the pre-set limit, rather that if they do business beyond the set limit, they will not be financed on the unapproved portion. Some factors will offer some limited finance against the level of unapproved invoices, providing the unapproved debts are well spread, although additional charges may be made to reflect the higher risk.

Under a recourse factoring arrangement, however, the credit limits set on customers are purely finance limits. Because the factor has very little to lose themselves if the client's customer ceases to trade, the limits set tend to be more flexible than those set by a non-recourse factor.

Although the factor will ultimately be concerned about their client's viability from suffering a bad debt, providing the client's ledger is well spread, the factor's security will not suffer. If a small bad debt is taken, the majority of their security, i.e. the remainder of the sales ledger, remains intact. Thus they will tend to be more liberal with their credit limits on their clients' customers, with more finance therefore offered.

As a halfway house, some non-recourse factors separate finance limits on customers and credit-approved limits, such that the client, in theory at least, gets maximum funding and credit protection at the same time. Equally, most factors will set discretionary limits, i.e. they will provide finance (and credit protection, if appropriate) automatically against a customer to a given level with no reference needing to be made to the factor.

Finally, commercial recourse factors will not set credit limits against a client's customers, providing the sales ledger is well spread. If the major customer does not represent more than 20–25% of the sales ledger and is unlikely to do so, the invoices are undisputed and less than 90 days past due, the CRF will generally fund the entire ledger at the agreed percentage. Whilst not setting finance limits per se, they will assess the top customers (usually over 10% of the sales ledger) and seek to discuss their findings with their clients to see whether commercially it is the right decision for the client to deal with that customer at such a high level.

Typically their standard levels of finance are 5–10% lower than their mainstream counterparts, but in general terms, 'what you see is what you get'.

Tips and traps – credit unapproved debts

When negotiating with the factoring companies:

Tips

- Check the levels of discretionary finance limits available on your customers – the higher they are the more finance will be made available.
- Check that the factor will finance unapproved debts as a matter of course.
- If looking at a non-recourse facility, will the non-recourse factor offer you finance limits separately from credit protection limits?
- If getting more than one quote, ask their representative to evaluate exactly how much cash will be generated from your existing sales ledger.
- Get a quote from a commercial recourse factor in addition to your other quotes and compare the ease of use and the actual level of finance likely to be made available.

Traps

- Most mainstream factors will not advance any monies against unapproved debts.
- If the factor does provide finance against unapproved invoices, they may seek to administer an additional charge.
- If there are no discretionary limits set on your customers, you may not know from day to day what your cash flow will be – see Chapter 7 for further details.

The spread of the customer base

Both recourse and non-recourse factors are concerned about the spread of a client's sales ledger. Under both facilities a threshold, expressed as a percentage of the sales ledger, will be set. If the client's major customer exceeds this threshold, any invoices in excess of the threshold will remain unfinanced.

Under a recourse factoring facility, the spread of the client's debtors is crucial to maintaining control, with the threshold notably less than those of non-recourse factors. In general terms, if the client enjoys an 80% prepayment facility, the threshold for the major customer will be determined by the size of the margin the recourse factor has in the outstanding sales ledger, in this case 20%. Theoretically, if the major customer failed, the factor would still have 80% of the client's ledger to rely upon. In very rare circumstances, unless the top customer was undoubted and/or the debt was credit insured externally, would the spread threshold exceed this margin.

Non-recourse factors, however, because they are providing bad debt protection against customers, are much closer to their client's major customer. Feeling more comfortable enables them to provide finance against a higher threshold, typically 30–35%. In certain situations this can be increased to 40–45%, and in extreme circumstances can be extended to as high as 60%.

Tips and traps – customer spread

Tips

- At the front end of a negotiation with the factors, negotiate the highest spread threshold you can – you may need it at a later stage. For their own control purposes and given your needs at that moment in time, the factor may seek to impose a low spread threshold. It is better to have a higher level already negotiated and drawn up in your agreement than to seek to renegotiate it at a later stage.
- Non-recourse factors are generally more generous than recourse factors on the spread of customers.
- Assess the viability of an external credit insurance policy – it should help the factor view the spread of customers more favourably.

Traps

- If using an external credit insurance policy, however, recourse factors will tend to stick to the credit limits set by the credit insurer in assessing the finance limits available on a given customer.

The ageing of outstanding invoices

Old debts will either be on their way to becoming bad debts or are in heavy dispute. Non-recourse and recourse factors treat the ageing of debts differently for funding purposes. Because the non-recourse factor is providing protection against bad debts, they will seek to pursue litigation against a customer if the debt is over 90 days past the due date.

However, because the debt has been approved by them, the factors will continue to fund the debt even though it is old. Certain non-recourse factors will automatically pay a client under their bad debt protection policy for the debt if it is 120 days old – regarding it as 'protracted default' by the customer.

Recourse factors, on the other hand, will withhold monies against invoices which are 90 days past due (some will look at only 60 days past due). Some will also levy additional refactoring charges to clients if customers debts are over the ageing threshold. Alternatively, the recourse factor will seek to reassign old debts back to a client – passing the responsibility for collection back to the client.

Tips and traps – the ageing of outstanding debts

Tips

- Check that the recourse factor will withhold funding against invoices after 90 days past due date and not 60 days past due.
- Check exactly when a non-recourse factor will pay out against an approved bad debt – upon notification of insolvency or after 120 days.

Traps

- Refactoring charges can vary between 0.5% and 1%, and will add to the costs of the facility.
- Watch out for reassignments, the responsibility for collection is passed back to you – ensure you are able to chase it effectively if this occurs, as the debt will be very old.

RECOURSE OR NON-RECOURSE?

The level of maximum funding generally depends upon the profile of your own sales ledger. If your sales ledger is well spread and ages well, i.e. only a small part of the ledger is more than 90 days past due, a recourse facility will typically provide the most funding, with a commercial recourse factor likely to generate the most funds.

If, however, you want the benefit of bad debt protection, as well as finance, you should check that the finance limits are set separately to the credit limits for approval.

The ideal facility in our experience has tended to be a commercial recourse factoring facility for the finance, using a separate credit insurance facility for the bad debt protection. Whilst presenting probably the most consistent cash flow, the overall package will be slightly more expensive than a non-recourse factoring solution (Table 8.1).

Table 8.1 Typical profiles of retentions for the three types of factors

Funding against	Non-recourse	Recourse	Commercial recourse
Spread	30–35%	20–25%	20–25%
Automatic approval of customers for financing purposes	typically £1k–5k	Equivalent to approximately 5% of the ledger	up to 20%
Disputes	Not financed	Not financed	Not financed
Ageing of debts	No retentions	>60/90 days	>60/90 days
Maximum (gross) funding	80–85%	75–80%	70–75%

INVOICE DISCOUNTING

Because of its higher perceived risk by the finance providers, as they have no relationship with the client's customers, invoice discounters will implement additional reporting restrictions. The discounter deals in paper, the client in goods and services. As a result, the discounter will finance according to their perception of the debts as reflected in the paperwork submitted to them. Without exception, clients operating an invoice discounting facility will be required to be able to produce the following information every month:

- aged debtors;
- management figures – profit and loss and balance sheet;
- reconciliation statement, linking the client's sales ledger to the discounters.

The four key security issues highlighted within the factoring section above are equally assessed within invoice discounting, although because invoice discounting is considered more risky the thresholds set tend to be lower. (Table 8.2.)

Table 8.2   Typical profiles of retentions for the three types of invoice discounters

Funding against	Agency factoring	Disclosed invoice discounting	Confidential invoice discounting
Spread	25–30%	20–25%	15–20%
Automatic approval of customers for financing purposes	typically £1k–5k	Equivalent to approximately 5% of the ledger	Equivalent to approximately 5% of the ledger
Disputes (derived from the discounter's audits)	Not financed	Not financed	Not financed
Ageing of debts	>60/90 days	>60/90 days	>60/90 days
Maximum (gross) funding	75–80%	75–80%	75–80%

As well as the issues of the individual activities of the operational side of the business, the discounters have a varied response upon the level of finance they will advance to a client.

THE FACILITY LIMIT

A factoring facility typically has no limit to the level of funds you can draw. The discounter, on the other hand, because they are not in direct control of the sales ledger, wants to ensure that they have some management control over their clients. To this end, they will typically set a fixed limit on the amount of finance they will make available to a client.

The fixed limit acts as a trigger mechanism for the discounters. It will only be hit if the sales ledger itself increases in size. At this stage, the discounter has to ascertain whether it is the positive reasons of increased sales growth or the negative reasons of worsening credit control or underlying problems with their security that have caused the limit to be hit.

Table 8.3 shows how if the client's credit control performance worsens, the fixed limit will be hit and additional finance will not be made available. Equally, if the client's turnover increased the limit would again be hit.

Table 8.3 Example

Client turnover	£4m	£4m	£5m
Net worth	£300k	£300k	£300k
Debt turn	62 days	75 days	62 days
Sales ledger	£800k	£965k	£998k
Discounter's advance rate (net)	75%	75%	75%
Notional maximum advance	£600k	£723k	£748k
Actual funds advanced	£600k	£650k	£650k
Fixed limit	£650k	£650k	£650k

At this stage the facility limit would need to be renegotiated. Given the latter case of increasing sales, providing the account has performed satisfactorily, it is likely to be nothing more than a formality. If it is weakened credit control by the client, the negotiations will be more difficult.

This initial limit will be set in line with a client's needs as demonstrated by their cash flow projections, and the likely level of debts to be discounted. It will typically also be set according to the level of net worth of the business, and a multiple thereof. Typically ranging from 2.5 to 3.5 times net worth, the facility is more generous than traditional banking (1:1), and indeed some discounters will finance a client without a net worth covenant.

Tips and traps – invoice discounting

Tips

- Check the multiple of net worth a discounter will allow as a funding line.
- Do not be too generous with the assumptions of credit control within your cash flow forecasts – the discounter may hold you to them.
- Arrange your computerised system to produce aged analyses on the basis of due date not invoice date – the over 90 day column will be a more accurate reflection of those debts which are actually over 90 days past due.
- Submit the required month-end information as soon as you can to the discounter – their department will have many clients to work on.

Traps

- When the auditors have completed their audit reports they may seek to recommend to their line managers that special retentions are made. Ensure the auditor tells you of these at the time of the audit such that you can plan your cash flow.

Summary

In order to get the most of your factoring facility, it is essential that you have a proactive approach towards the factoring company you use. We have enclosed as an appendix to this chapter a checklist which will help you to determine which factor will offer you the most finance and flexibility from your factoring facility. Remember, no two factors are the same!

Checklist to negotiate maximum funding from a factoring facility

Recourse factoring

What maximum spread restriction will the factor allow?			_____ %

When does the factor disapprove your debts for age?   30___   60___   90___ days

past due?

Does the factor impose finance limits on your customers?	Yes _____	No _____

If yes, what is the discretionary limit set for any customer?   £_____

Will the factor finance unapproved debts?	Yes _____	No _____

If you have an external credit insurance policy will they finance to your credit insured limits only	Yes _____	No _____

Non-recourse factoring

What maximum spread restriction will the factor allow?		_____ %

When does the factor pay out for bad debts?   120 ___   150___ days

Upon notification of insolvency of the customer   ____?

Does the factor limit the level of finance provided to the credit limits set on your customers?	Yes _____	No _____

What is the discretionary limit set for any customer?   £_____

What are the conditions attached to this discretion?   _____

Will the factor finance
unapproved debts?   Yes _____   No _____

Invoice discounting

What maximum spread
threshold will the
discounter allow?   _____ %

When does the
discounter disapprove
your debts for age?   30___   60___   90___ days

                                                        past due?

Does the discounter
impose finance limits on
your customers?   Yes _____   No _____

If yes, what is the
discretionary limit set for
any customer?   _____

Will the discounter
finance unapproved debts?   Yes _____   No _____

If you have an external
credit insurance policy
will they finance to your
credit insured limits only   Yes _____   No _____

_____

Chapter 9

Choosing a factor

For companies that feel they could benefit from using a factoring or invoice discounting service there can be a lot of services to choose from. The breadth of choice is dependent upon how well the company meets the general selection criteria of the industry, the number of factors approached, the packaging of the proposal and what sort of factor the company wants as a partner. In this chapter we seek to make choosing the best factor easier. Here we give the guidelines on how to assess what they want and can expect from a factor. Chapter 10 details the next stage of selecting a factor.

Choosing a factor or invoice discounter is not simply one of selecting the cheapest – this is especially important where factoring is concerned and the level of service is a major feature of the facility.

FOR MANY IT IS A BUYERS' MARKET

At the time of writing there are over 60 factors and discounters in the UK. It is feasible that companies with a product preferred by the industry, for example a temporary recruitment agency, could obtain an offer from all 60 or so in the market. Companies with an average product, a mixed quality of debtors, etc. may potentially get offers from 10 or more. Having said that, those in what are viewed as marginal industries or with weak financials, track record and management may find it hard to obtain offers at all.

THE IMPORTANCE OF THE RIGHT CHOICE

Factoring agreements are generally not that difficult to terminate. However, even if you choose a factor which requires no notice period, having to change will cause you disruption and inconvenience.

Prudent selection is vital to ensure you secure the best facility at the right price. The more research you do beforehand, the more satisfied you are likely to be. An example of one company who was caught out by not knowing enough about how factoring works is a company in the Midlands who were delighted to find a factor with a regional service office nearby. Only when the facility was in use did the client discover that only certain types of enquiries were handled locally. Questions regarding cash advances had to be phoned through to the head office two hundred miles away.

IDENTIFYING WHAT IS BEST FOR YOUR COMPANY

Factoring is a finance and administration tool which may help your company achieve its goals. If you can define what goals these are in the short and medium term – three years – you can more easily work out exactly what you will need from a factoring or invoice discounting facility.

Use cash-flow forecasts to calculate the amount of working capital you expect to need. Will it be replacing your existing overdraft? Will you require bad debt protection or credit insurance cover? Will you downsize your own sales ledger department?

What should a factoring or invoice discounting facility include?

Are you looking purely for a source of finance or for credit management and bad debt protection too? Use the following checklist of features of factoring facilities to ascertain what would be most suitable for your company.

- finance;
- ability to draw cash whenever needed without penalty;
- bad debt protection;
- credit risk assessment of customers;
- a collections service with or without your active involvement;
- ability to control your own collections;
- foreign currency accounting;
- export collections service;
- on-line management information system;
- on-line transmission of invoices to the factor.

What sort of partner?

Now, with a clear idea of what is needed from the facility itself one can work out what overall considerations will affect your choice of the provider of that facility apart from price. In general, the smaller the factor, the better position you will have in negotiating any changes in procedure, extra financing for example. You are more likely to know at least one of the factor's directors and will be able to approach him or her directly with a query. Directors are often personally involved in the negotiation stage and their commitment to or refusal to make an offer in principle can usually be achieved at the first meeting with them.

In terms of philosophy the smaller factors are generally headed up by fellow small-business people who share their clients' entrepreneurial spirit.

One word of warning – over the past three years a number of factoring and discounting houses have departed from the market, and whilst the majority have been controlled exits with their portfolios bought by another factor, the receivership of London and Provincial Factors caused temporary problems for some clients. Always check the factor's own financial status by looking at their accounts. Remember that the factoring and discounting industry is not regulated by the Bank of England.

On the other hand if your company chooses a larger factor it will be able to progress from full service factoring to disclosed discounting to confidential invoice discounting as it grows without changing factor. Most larger factors also provide export services and foreign currency accounting. It has to be said that changing facility even within the same factoring house will necessitate a new agreement and different teams will take over the management of the account.

Elements to consider when assessing the relative merits of various factors are:

- Will becoming a client of the factoring subsidiary of your bank be advantageous to you?
- Is it important that they are located near enough to discuss issues in person?
- Is there easy access to a director?
- Do you prefer to be a client of a major organisation, with the backing of a clearing bank?
- Is there evidence of their ability to collect effectively in your industry sector?
- Is the termination period acceptable?
- If the factor has a regional office will all your queries be handled here or will you have to contact their head office?

OBTAINING OFFERS

The broker

Help can be obtained from a factoring broker but check beforehand that the broker is not tied to a particular factoring company. Links to the factoring company may be in the form of sponsorship. Having established that the broker is independent one can feel confident that he or she will be acting in the interests of the client. The broker's charges are usually paid by the incoming factor, however, there may be an extra charge in the case of companies which are particularly difficult to place.

The accountant

Ask your accountant for advice on whom to approach. First determine the accountant's level of familiarity with the facilities and the market, the number of factoring companies or invoice discounters he or she has dealt with and any examples of satisfied clients.

The accountant may charge you for this exercise. Commissions are usually payable by the factor to accountants who introduce business. This commission may meet the cost of the accountant's involvement. It is worth considering combining the efforts of the independent broker and the accountant with the broker making the initial approaches to suitable factors and the accountant advising at final negotiation stage, once offers in principle have been obtained. Brokers and accountants will be able to advise on the financial security of the factors approached.

The bank manager

Ascertain the manager's breadth of knowledge of the factoring and invoice discounting market as a whole. Check what commission, actual or notional, the bank manager's branch stands to gain by introducing you to the in-house factor. If the bank concerned does not have its own factoring subsidiary still check what commissions are payable for an introduction to another factor, if any. The payment of commissions is not wrong, but knowing of their existence may help clients to make a better decision. See also Chapter 15.

Your own efforts

Obtain a list of factoring companies from the ABF&D and the AIF. The contact phone numbers of these two organisations are given in the reference section of this book. A list of factors and invoice discounters is also printed each month in the magazine *Business Money*. There are over 50 UK-based companies offering factoring and around 30 offering discounting. Larger ones are generally subsidiaries of banks and members of the Association of British Factors and Discounters. Some smaller factoring houses belong to the Association of Invoice Factors. Both of the above have their own code of conduct. There are others which are not affiliated to either organisation.

Your bank manager and your accountant may encourage you to use the in-house factor but you should take a purely commercial view and shop around for the best service available for your company. The in-house factor could be the best factor for you, but you should arrive at your decision after due examination of what else is on offer.

Estimating the value, savings and cost

A useful exercise to complete before entering negotiations is to make an estimate of what you will save by using a factor, what you stand to gain in terms of new opportunities and what you would be prepared to pay for a facility that afforded you these same savings and opportunities. As with any cost/benefit analysis this will help you focus on the value of a facility rather than viewing it purely as an add-on cost. This will also assist you during negotiations when factoring salespeople may overestimate the potential savings and benefits of their services. You will also have a better idea of the maximum feasible price for such a facility.

Figure 6.1 will give you an indication of what you can save by using a factor and the opportunity value to your firm of having access to extra funding. Calculate the costs that your company has incurred over the last twelve months.

Tie-break – the nitty-gritty

When you have shortlisted potential factors and have been offered the basic elements of the service you want, e.g. bad debt protection, collections, etc. you may find the following useful in finally selecting which is best for you.

Try the following to help differentiate:

- Speak to clients already using a particular factor.
- Meet the factor's personnel who will be delivering the service, e.g. credit underwriters, credit managers, collection staff, client managers.
- Look at debt turn achieved in your industry sector, beware that you compare like with like (some factors may include the debt turn of their invoice discounting clients in their overall figures, ask for statistics excluding this).
- Will the factor telephone chase for 'small amounts' – how small?
- Is every debtor phoned?
- Are the chasing procedures suitable for your business?
- Can you chase some of your own debts if required?

Summary

Through preparation and knowing what the factors are looking for you could be in a stronger negotiating position. Chapter 10 explains in more detail how to approach this. However, in general terms, treat the factors and invoice discounters with the same respect you would any potential investor in your company. They are in the risk business, specialising in 'book debt finance' and will be looking at the security of their potential investment and an 'exit route'.

Factors like businesses have:

- up-to-date accounts, including management accounts;
- good management;
- proven products or services;
- a future and are planning for it;

- financial investment by the client's directors;
- paid-up preferential creditors;
- a good spread of customers (though some factors will finance against high concentrations).

Factors generally look in great detail at a prospective client before agreeing to invest. Make sure your accounts are in order and up to date and always answer the factor's questions fully. Reconcile your sales ledger before meeting them and don't give them any nasty surprises. Prepare a forecast for at least the year ahead. The information the factor needs to assess whether to make an offer of a facility is basically that included in the funding profile in Figure 9.1.

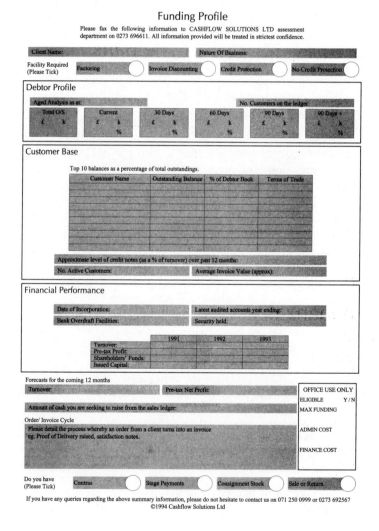

Figure 9.1 Funding profile

Chapter 10

How to negotiate the facility

Once the decision to factor has been made, it is now necessary to go through the time-consuming and laborious process of negotiating the facility. Negotiations for a standard factoring facility will last around 3–4 weeks in total from start to finish, with 12 stages to the negotiation typically seen. If a proactive approach is taken to the process, this will save substantial time as well as generating competitively costed facilities.

In negotiating the best facility, it is essential to understand not only the mechanics of raising factoring finance, but also what is motivating the parties involved within the whole process. Earlier we examined the technical issues facing the factors in their assessment of the suitability of a potential client company. In practice, however, it is two key individuals from the factoring companies who hold the key to actually finalising the facility – the business development manager (BDM) and the surveyor.

THE BDM's ROLE

Selling factoring and invoice discounting to a prospective client is easy.
It's selling the proposition 'in-house' that is difficult!

This is a familiar statement from most of the BDMs within the factoring industry, and brings us to the first essential point to recognise. Almost without exception, the BDM's who first visit a prospective client have no actual decision-making capacity. Instead, they will act as filters for proposals received, rejecting unsuitable applicants at an early stage. Their role is principally one of co-ordination, of collating information for presentation to the decision-making collective – the credit committee.

Like most salespeople they will be targeted to perform. Generally speaking, the industry targets its sales staff to generate around two new clients per month. At first, this might not appear to be a hard target to achieve. However, if one considers that on average only about one in ten generated leads is actually taken on as a client, there can be a great deal of time wasted in achieving the set targets.

The BDM's role is a difficult one. It is like walking a tightrope. On the one hand, selling their factoring company and its associated added value to a client company and their advisors, and on the other, ensuring their own credit committee will support the client. The conflict between sales and credit departments is as old as commerce itself, but when the sales activity involves the provision of finance, the role of the 'credit underwriters' is even more important.

The twelve negotiation stages detailed in Figure 10.1 highlight the key role that the factors' BDMs have in co-ordinating the negotiation process, in satisfying all parties concerned. Their role, however, is vital to the negotiation process. The decision makers will not actually see the potential client's business, nor will they meet its directors.[1] Instead they will see the filtered presentations made to them by their respective BDMs and their other staff member, the surveyor, who will visit a potential client's premises.

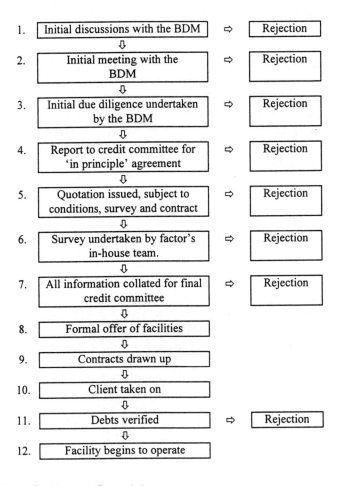

Figure 10.1   The 12 stages of negotiation

From initial contact established over the telephone with the factor's BDMs (1), the factor makes a brief assessment of whether they can assist. A meeting will be arranged to formalise their initial appraisal (2). Summary financial information will be requested ahead of the initial meeting:

- audited accounts for the last three years trading;
- up-to-date management figures;
- aged debtors analysis for the previous month end;
- projections for the coming 12 months – profit and loss and a linked cash flow projection;
- summary marketing information on the client company;
- a completed proposal form.

Armed with this information, the BDM can then assess in principle whether the client company will be accepted by the board of directors. From the initial meeting, the BDM will make his or her assessment of the quality of the business and its management, closely cross-questioning their respective backgrounds.

The factor then undertakes their initial due diligence (3), carrying out research in the following areas:

- the credit standing of the company – checking for any adverse credit history – County Court Judgements (CCJs), etc.;
- the credit standing of the company directors – personal searches are taken on the directors of the company, again checking for any adverse credit history;[2]
- the Companies House registers to obtain details of any other directorships held by the prospective client's management, with further research undertaken if associate companies, current or historic, are found.

The aim of the initial due diligence is to generate facts which require further explanation and information, which could compromise the provision of a facility.

Once the initial due diligence has been undertaken, a brief summary report is presented through to their underwriters for an 'in principle' agreement to progress matters further (4). From initial underwriter satisfaction, an initial quote will be raised (5), which will include various conditions of acceptance, and a survey of the books of the company.

The survey (6) is undertaken typically by an in-house member of staff,[3] whose principal task is to validate the information supplied by the client and the BDM. Normally taking less than a day, it involves a closer appraisal of the prospective client's financial position and the quality of the security for the factor. The surveyor will examine:

- the sales day book – to validate turnover figures and to see the incidence of credit notes;
- historic aged debtors analyses – to analyse the profile of the ledger: size of

major customer, debts over 90 days past due, bad debts over the previous six months, etc.;

- details of any contracts – to see the underlying terms of trade;
- the order/invoice cycle – to examine the paper trail that lies behind invoices raised, e.g. purchase order through to proof of delivery;
- the bank statements – to note how the account has been performing: the swinging of the account in and out of credit and the incidence of any bounced cheques;
- the purchase ledger – to see the incidence of creditor pressure and any major supplier's terms and conditions which may compromise the factor's security, e.g. severe retention of title clauses;
- details of the preferential creditors – VAT and PAYE;
- the cash book.

At the end of the survey, the surveyor should be able to pinpoint any specific questions requiring answers and discuss any issues which may influence the factor's decision to progress matters further.

THE SURVEYOR'S ROLE

The surveyor is perhaps the most important person to influence. It is they who collate all the information for final presentation to the factor's credit committee (7), the ultimate decision makers. In most cases, the BDM will not be present at the credit committee presentation to act on a client company's behalf. The surveyor will therefore be presenting the case on behalf of the client company, whilst ensuring the factor's position is protected at the same time.

This role is not an easy one, presenting the case to a team of 5–7 senior managers each of whom will have an opinion on the proposition being assessed, and the comments the surveyor may have made in their report. The surveyor can easily feel intimidated by a group of senior managers and if their arguments are not watertight they will be torn apart. As a result, the surveyor has to feel totally convinced and comfortable with everything presented, so as to make an effective case to their credit committee.

THE CREDIT COMMITTEE

The depth and breadth of the decision making process will typically depend upon the value of the investment. Within certain factoring companies some underwriting authority has filtered down to individual senior managers within the operational side of the business. Most, however, still adopt a collective approach to underwriting. Whilst varying from factor to factor, any proposed investment in excess of £250 000 will almost certainly need to go before a collective body of 'in-house' underwriters – the 'credit committee'.

Usually comprised of at least one board director and around five in-house individuals taken from different areas of operation from within the business, the credit committee will assess a given proposition as a collective. Each person within the committee will have their own specialist expertise (and prejudices) and will tend to look at a given proposition from that viewpoint. The credit committee will look at the information presented by:

- the client
- the client's advisors[4]
- the BDM
- the surveyor

seeking to critically assess each proposition on its own merits. As a result, the factor, via the credit committee, will tend to take a balanced view of propositions presented.

From the credit committee a decision is made, with various conditions attached, which enables a formal offer of facilities to be made to the client (8). Once accepted, contracts are drawn up (9), with preparation then made to take the client on (10).

THE TAKE-ON

Once all the paperwork has been completed and all the necessary conditions of support satisfied, the client is ready to start. At this point, all details of the client's outstanding sales ledger are transferred on to the factor's computer system. Once everything is satisfactory, the facility is formally made available and the client then starts to enjoy the benefits the facility can offer (12).

REJECTION

At any stage of the negotiation process, the factor may reject an application if there is information available which either compromises the factor's security or makes them feel uncomfortable about the financing of the business or the directors. This can even extend to the take-on, when negotiations have finished.

As part of the factor's audit procedures, the invoices taken on are verified by the factor's in-house collections staff, to confirm that the invoices are undisputed and that goods have been delivered in accordance with the customers' requests.

It is even at this stage that some client companies have been rejected. If, for example, the customers who have been telephoned reveal substantial trading disputes, stage payments or other features the factors do not feel comfortable with and which were contrary to their initial agreement with the client, they may still be rejected.

THE 'STOOL EFFECT'

Using the analogy of a four-legged stool, it is possible to generate an approximate idea of whether a given proposition will be supported. The legs of the stool are the quality issues in the factor's risk assessment:

● financial – the profitability and net worth of the prospect;
● commercial – the industry and the terms of trade;
● security – the quality and spread of the customers;
● management – the current performance and history of the client's management.

The stool requires at least three legs to stand up. If one of the above quality issues is weak in a given proposition, one leg disappears. If there are two, the chances of support are dramatically minimised, unless there are mitigating circumstances surrounding one of the issues.

For example, if a prospect is currently profitable but has a negative net worth and the security offered to the factoring company is good, the proposition is likely to be supported. If, however, the previous company had failed with an unresolved liability to the previous bankers and the major customer comprised 70% of the sales ledger, very few factors would support the proposition.

ADVERSE CREDIT HISTORY

The issue of adverse credit history is a difficult issue to handle. Instinctively perhaps many potential clients have tried to hide adverse credit information, believing that if it is 'swept under the carpet' no-one will find out. However, as Oscar Wilde once said: 'Confidence is like virginity – you lose it only once!'

In our experience of raising factoring finance, we have come across ongoing factoring relationships which have been terminated as a direct result of undisclosed facts coming to light which were not disclosed at the time of initial appraisal. Trust is crucial for a factoring relationship to work – it is at the very centre of the financial relationship.

Disclosing adverse information up front demonstrates greater integrity and is more likely to be rewarded. Most skeletons in the cupboard, such as previous liquidations and corporate or personal County Court Judgements (CCJs), can be overcome, providing any adverse credit information has been 'ethical' and there are not likely to be any issues directly affecting the business in the future, e.g. a director being made personally bankrupt by a previous bank guarantee.

COMPETITIVE QUOTES

The marketplace is comprised of around 62 different providers of factoring and invoice discounting facilities. As a result, the marketplace is highly competitive. For good quality business – that which is profitable and has a clean factorable product – highly competitive quotes can be sourced.

Our experience shows that the ideal number of competitive quotes to get is three. Any more and the individual BDMs lose interest as their individual chances of getting the business do not justify the amount of work needed to get the proposition into a manageable position for sanction by their credit committee. Any less and the quotes may not fully suit an individual company's needs.

However, if three competitive quotes are obtained, an extensive amount of time can be spent in dealing with the business issue, as each separate negotiation takes about 2–3 days of senior management time.

In part this explains the development of the emerging specialist factoring and invoice discounting brokers, who use their industry knowledge to collate information into packages as seen from the factoring company's point of view. This not only saves a great deal of time for the prospective client management, but also enables the BDM to cut through a lot of the administrative red tape to get agreements in principle at an earlier stage. Equally it gives the prospective client company the 'inside track' on many factors and the benefit of some of the 'tricks of the trade', which can save time and money.

GETTING THE BEST RESULT

The client company deals in goods and services, whereas the factor deals in paper and risk. Because the key decision makers do not actually meet the prospective client, it is necessary to influence the 'ivory tower' decision makers by means of the information supplied, while at the same time directly influencing the BDM and the surveyor.

The professional BDM will want to do business and will seek to do what is realistically necessary to achieve that goal and, as a result, will be positive towards generating a solution to a client's needs. The surveyor on the other hand is not involved within the sales culture on a day-to-day basis and, being more involved in the operational side of the business, tends to be more conservative in approach, having a role more akin to a gamekeeper.

It is necessary therefore to make the lives of both the BDM and the surveyor as easy as possible to generate positive results. By presenting a complete picture of the client company in summary form, the key factoring personnel's jobs are made easier, reducing the time they need to spend presenting their findings and speeding up the decision-making process.

SOME OF THE 'TRICKS OF THE TRADE'

From our experience of broking factoring and invoice discounting propositions, there are a number of inside tricks of the trade, which will help in the sourcing of factoring finance:

- Type the factor's proposal form. The proposal forms summarise much of the statutory information. Probably 95% of proposal forms submitted to the factoring companies are in a handwritten format. The 'ivory tower' decision makers see all proposal forms together with the other collated information. By being typed, the proposition generates an air of professionalism, increasing its profile.
- Fully reconcile the sales ledger before a member of the survey team arrives to undertake their due diligence. Unallocated cash can indicate a lack of control.
- Chase up any old invoices vigorously and duly reconcile any bad debts taken. The factors will focus upon the over-90-day column.
- Critically analyse the order/invoice cycle to see if it is watertight. If it can be tightened up without compromising the running of the business, then think about ways of doing so.
- If there are any skeletons in the cupboard, e.g. previous liquidations, corporate or personal County Court Judgements (CCJs), it is better to be up front about them and look towards explaining how they occurred and why they will not materialise again.
- If there are any CCJs that have been registered but paid, get them 'satisfied' by the respective courts in which the action took place before the negotiations take place.

Summary

The negotiation process is very similar to raising any form of finance, although the factors tend to get more involved in their due diligence, undertaking a survey of the company's books. The key issues to focus upon relate to who actually makes the decision and who plays the key role in influencing those decisions. Make their jobs easier and the chances of success are greatly enhanced.

Checklist for negotiating a facility

Financial information required

Last three year's audited accounts

Up-to-date management figures

Projections for the coming 12 months   – Profit and Loss
                                        – Cash flow

Aged debtors analysis for previous month end

Aged creditors analysis for previous month end

General tips

Vigorously chase very old debts

Fully reconcile the outstanding sales ledger

Type the factor's proposal form

Put together a summary of the business activities

Put together CVs of executive directors

Disclose full information to the BDM and surveyor

Examine your order/invoice cycle – if it can be tightened, do it

Adverse credit information

Get any County Court Judgements on the business satisfied

Get any County Court Judgements on the directors satisfied

If previous company failure – get liquidator's report

NOTES

1 The exception to this rule is generally restricted to the smaller factors, where the directors perform the business development role. Equally, if the prospective client represents a larger facility to the mainstream factor, a director may meet the client in an attempt to positively influence the prospective client's decision to take up a facility with them.

2 The philosophy behind the personal searches is that if company directors cannot look after their personal credit, how will they perform with corporate credit?

3 A number of factors have filtered some authority down to the BDMs to undertake their own surveys up to a certain projected level of funds invested. Equally, one factor does not undertake surveys on factoring clients, instead relying upon telephone verification of the invoices when the facility commences.

4 If the proposition has come from a known good source of business, e.g. a specialist factoring broker of good standing or a known quality accountant it will add weight to the consideration of the proposition.

Chapter 11

Invoice discounting and the MBO

The leveraged buyout (LBO), management buyout (MBO) and acquisition culture of the eighties has long been relegated to the corporate history books, as recession steadily focused corporate minds upon survival. The invoice discounting industry played a very active role in supporting this culture, and as recession begins to ease its role will be reinforced once more.

As the large corporates begin to review their financing strategies to take advantage of the opportunities the recovery will bring, we should expect to see an increase in the number of MBOs being seen. Corporate bankers will maintain their cautious approach, which will focus the minds of the corporate finance directors towards divesting groups of underperforming subsidiaries.

The role of the MBO has been the focus of many individual books and it is not proposed to examine the finer points of effecting an MBO, rather to look instead upon how the invoice discounting industry[1] can and has been used to assist with the financing of the activity.

In order to appraise the reader of how the facilities can assist the financing of an MBO, appreciation needs to be seen of some of the financial benefits of invoice discounting that can be harnessed.

INVOICE DISCOUNTING AND THE MBO

With most MBOs, the level of finance available from the MBO team themselves will typically prove insufficient to finance the whole transaction, especially as the size of the transaction increases. As a result, other sources of finance need to be found, with a mixture of debt, equity and mezzanine finance likely.

There are commercial benefits to the MBO team in sourcing debt rather than equity. The more debt that is sourced, the less equity needs to be given away to external financiers. Equally, providing interest rates remain low for the term of the borrowing, the return on capital employed can increase markedly, the philosophy behind so many of the leveraged buyouts in the eighties.

If increased debt is the key financial strategy for an MBO, invoice discounting can provide a material part of that debt requirement. The discounter can provide up to 85% against book debts as compared to 30–50% from traditional banking. Equally, given the MBO team will most likely have to remortgage their own personal properties or other assets in order to fund their own injection of cash in the transaction, additional bank funding may prove difficult to raise in view of the reduced security available.

Furthermore, by the very nature of the MBO team taking over an existing business, albeit underperforming, the incoming team will have the ambition and drive to push the acquired business forward. As a result, expansion will typically follow an MBO, which will require further working capital finance, the natural domain of sales-linked finance.

STRUCTURING THE FINANCING OF THE MBO

The invoice discounting industry can play an active part in assisting with the financing of the MBO, with the essential element relating to the initial payment released when the facility commences. Whilst providing the ongoing working capital facilities to support the MBO team, on the first day of an invoice discounting facility a lump sum is released from the outstanding sales ledger (excluding any export invoices), in accordance with the factor's given advance rate within the financing package. To this end, typically around 70% will be released against the outstanding book debts, with for example around £840k being released from a ledger of £1.2m.

Using the initial funding from invoice discounting, the equity stakes taken by the external parties can be dramatically reduced. However, from the equity providers' point of view, it presents a double-edged sword; whilst giving them greater comfort as their risk capital is reduced, they are presented with a lower dividend flow.

EXAMPLES OF TECHNIQUES FOR USING INVOICE DISCOUNTING TO SUPPORT AN MBO TRANSACTION

Note of caution: The following scenarios are examples of techniques which have been implemented in practice within the invoice discounting and factoring industries to support MBOs, acquisitions and MBIs. Whilst they have been carefully structured by the respective invoice discounters and factors, readers are strongly advised to seek professional legal advice in regards the structuring of such transactions, to ensure full compliance with the Companies Act 1985, with special consideration paid to the issue of financial assistance.

Suppose a company that is subject to an MBO has a turnover of £3.5m, net assets of £500k, an outstanding sales ledger of £732k (i.e. debt turn of about

65 days) and historic audited pre-tax net profits of £100k. Suppose the proposed purchase price is seven times historic earnings, i.e. £700k. The incoming management are investing £100k of their own funds together with an external equity investment of £200k.

Scenario 1: pre-acquisition financing

Day before acquisition

On the day before the MBO takes place, the target company discounts its invoices. Working on the basis that the factor advances a net 70% (after retentions) against invoices, they will be able to release 70% of the target's outstanding sales ledger balance. Upon invoice discounting about £512k is generated into the target's cash flow.

Using these funds, the target company pays the outgoing shareholders a dividend of £400k, directly reducing the target's net asset value to £100k. As a result, on the date of purchase the proposed consideration of £700k is reduced to £300k.

Day of acquisition

On the day of acquisition the remaining consideration, £300k, is paid out of external equity, £200k and £100k of the management's stake.

There is residual capital of £112k from invoice discounting, which with the ongoing facility will provide ongoing working capital to fund the expansion plans of the MBO team.

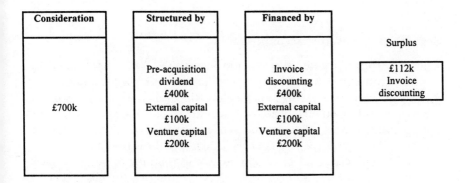

Figure 11.1   The financial structure of pre-acquisition financing

Scenario 2: post-acquisition financing

Figure 11.2 highlights the structure of post-acquisition financing. On the day before the acquisition takes place, the purchaser instructs a 'friendly' bank to advance an unsecured bridging loan of £400k to assist with the financing of the acquisition, with the loan being repaid on day 1 of the transaction. The consideration of £700k is the paid directly out of the bridging loan of £400k, together with the external venture capital, £200k, and the incoming management's capital of £100k.

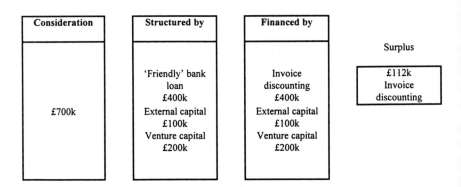

Figure 11.2   The financial structure of post-acquisition financing

On the day after the MBO, the acquired company discounts its invoices releasing cash flow of approximately £512k from its invoices on the first day of invoice discounting. This is then used to immediately repay the bank loan of £400k, again leaving a residual balance of £112k, together with the ongoing facilities to enable the working capital requirement of the team to be mostly satisfied.

Scenario 3: the escrow account

Figure 11.3 demonstrates the scenario increasingly being used when the invoice discounting finance is provided prior to the MBO taking place. Immediately prior to the MBO taking place, the incoming invoice discounter releases funds into an escrow account with the target's solicitors, but held to the discounter's favour. The acquisition takes place with the funds released to the purchaser once the debts have been assigned to the discounter.

Most discounters prefer to provide invoice discounting or factoring facilities once the MBO has actually taken place. In this way, the discounter has an easier role to fulfil, just that of providing finance, rather than taking into consideration any complications relating to the Companies Act.

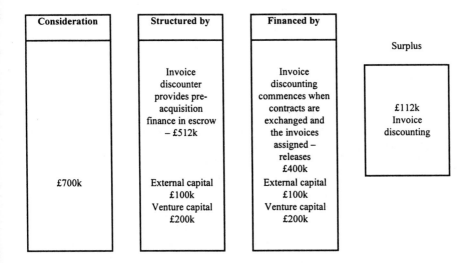

Consideration	Structured by	Financed by
	Invoice discounter provides pre-acquisition finance in escrow – £512k	Invoice discounting commences when contracts are exchanged and the invoices assigned – releases £400k
£700k	External capital £100k Venture capital £200k	External capital £100k Venture capital £200k

Surplus

£112k Invoice discounting

Figure 11.3 The financial structure of post-acquisition financing using the escrow account

FINANCIAL CONSIDERATIONS

In looking towards using the initial injection of cash flow released directly from the commencement of the invoice discounting facilities, invoice discounters will critically appraise the projections of a client company. For whilst traditionally short-term finance should finance short-term assets by using invoice discounting, current assets are being used to finance what is ostensibly a longer-term investment profile. Thus using invoice discounting to finance an MBO requires that the underlying cash flow of the business can sustain a downturn in business. As a result, discounters tend to focus heavily on the cash flow of the business to see what 'headroom',[2] if any, exists.

INVOICE DISCOUNTERS' PREFERENCES

Acquisitions tend to present higher-risk propositions to the acquirees and discounters alike, with so many unforeseen issues materialising only after the acquisition has been made. As a result, MBOs are particularly favoured by the industry as a whole. With the existing management already familiar with the company and its culture, the chances of success are generally greater and the perceived risks by the discounters less.

As a result of this favoured view, a number of the factors and discounters have set up specialist divisions to cater for the MBO market. With so many

MBOs being time sensitive, speed of action and flexibility are essential to satisfy a vendor's wishes.

PACKAGED FINANCE AND MBOS

As seen earlier, some factors and discounters are now able to support their core invoice discounting facility with additional finance secured on other assets. In regards an MBO transaction, this can be particularly beneficial, enabling a further reduction in the level of external equity participation. The further increased debt, however, potentially exposes the post MBO business to the higher inherent risks associated with increased levels of gearing. As seen all too often with the leveraged buyouts of the 1980s, higher interest rates together with a downturn in business levels can have disastrous results for the serviceability of high levels of debt with the very survival of the business potentially brought into question.

MBO case study

One of the leading exponents of the packaged finance facility, TSB Commercial Finance Ltd, regard the contingencies of the cash flow projections as central to their assessment of a given proposal in determining whether they will provide financial support. As their marketing director, Murray Chisholm explains:

> The cash flow should always be modelled to look at contingencies, gross profit failing to meet expectations, debt turn increasing or creditor payable term decreasing, all of which will have an effect on the cash flow requirement of the business. In this way, any peaks in cash flow could be facilitated through a 'top-up' facility, funding against stock and fixed assets.

Starting with current assets, their approach is to provide an invoice discounting facility against UK debtors and where appropriate export debtors, and to meet seasonal peaks in cash-flow requirement by providing a stock finance facility against finished stock. As Mr Chisholm continues:

> Generally an invoice discounting facility would provide up to 85% advance against debtors and a stock finance facility up to 30% advance against finished stock. Term loans against plant and machinery or buildings could also be provided by taking specific security against fixed assets and funding these on a term basis.

TSB were approached by a management team seeking to buy a textile manufacturer out of receivership. Being too small for a Venture Capitalist, a combination of directors' equity, bank overdraft facilities and packaged finance enabled the incoming team to meet the purchase consideration and have sufficient working capital facilities to develop the business.

Purchase consideration	£200k
Directors' equity	£100k
Shortfall in purchase consideration	£100k

Bank overdraft requirement	£100k
Working capital requirement	£650k
Bank overdraft secured on directors' houses and personal guarantees	£100k
Packaged finance	£650k

This latter packaged finance facility was met by 80% against debtors on a confidential invoice discounting facility together with a standby facility secured on finished goods stock.

LEVERAGED BUYOUTS (LBOS)

In the 1980s, the leverage buyout (LBO) culture was imported into the UK. 'Bootstrap' LBOs became prevalent, where the entire purchase consideration was met from using the target's assets to support the borrowing requirement. In many cases, the buyer did not use their own funds to assist with the purchase, other than the professional fees incurred. In this way, the acquired company was 'picked up by its own bootstraps'.[3]

The culture of LBOs has long since gone as recession increased interest rates, resulting in many LBO financed companies at best struggling to meet their interest burden, or at worst failing.

Given the inherent high risks associated with LBOs, it is unlikely that an invoice discounter would support an MBO without the existing management injecting some of their own cash, although the level of gearing tolerated is certainly markedly more favourably supported than that of traditional banking – 100% gearing.

Summary

We have seen that the invoice discounting industry can play a key role within the MBO culture in seeking by providing:

- sufficient debt finance to satisfy a team's immediate objective of having minimum involvement from equity holders;
- flexibility of additional finance that grows with the management's ambitions;
- a higher rate of return on capital invested, in stable economic conditions.

NOTES

1 Invoice discounting will be used in this section as the generic term for both factoring and invoice discounting. MBOs and acquisitions because of their size tend to be the domain of the invoice discounters.
2 i.e. does the MBO team require full funding?
3 Sidney Rutberg 'Where do we go from here? *The Secured Lender* magazine, June 1994, p.46.

Chapter 12

Factoring developments in international markets

The modern factoring industry has evolved from its roots within the textile industries of the USA. The provision of finance against accounts receivables first began in the 1890s, with the first link between the banking sector and factors being seen as early as 1919 under the auspices of the banking laws of the state of New York.

However, industry growth, both domestically in the US and elsewhere, was slow to take off with only a handful of bank-supported factors operating in the early 1960s.

The industry did not spread into the remaining world economies until the 1960s, with the first factoring company founded in the UK in 1960. Since then, the factoring industry has grown markedly throughout the world, with more than 750 factoring companies now operating in 44 different countries, servicing approximately 116 000 companies and their sales to over 6 500 000 customers.[1]

MARKET TRENDS – WORLD-WIDE

Table 12.1 highlights that almost all the developed economies have factoring facilities available for both domestic and export business, with facilities beginning to evolve in an increasing number of developing countries.

The world-wide market continues to demonstrate growth. As Table 12.2 demonstrates, over the period 1980–1993 the market grew by 390%, averaging 12.58% per annum (FCI 1994). Such underlying levels of growth demonstrate that factoring world-wide is becoming increasingly recognised as a beneficial financial tool to fund expansion.

Whilst underlying growth has been consistent, as the world economy slowed during the period 1990–1993 so the overall levels of factoring turnover fell. With the largest factoring markets – USA and most of Europe – having been in recession, the levels of business activity in those countries were directly affected, as well as those supplier countries relying upon their sales to the western economies.

Table 12.1 World-wide factoring figures: factoring volume by country in 1993 in $m

Number of companies*	Continent	Domestic	International	Total
	Europe			
3	Austria	1 710	123	1 833
7	Belgium	2 800	1 200	4 000
2	Cyprus	145	7	152
2	Czech Republic	87	88	175
6	Denmark	1 360	260	1 620
4	Finland	1 972	28	2 000
21	France	15 700	1 200	16 900
17	Germany	9 300	2 000	11 300
6	Hungary	10	50	60
1	Iceland	0	22	22
4	Ireland	2 090	15	2 105
75	Italy	50 250	1 300	51 550
1	Luxembourg	10	10	20
5	Netherlands	8 000	3 000	11 000
10	Norway	2 260	140	2 400
11	Portugal	2 050	62	2 112
20	Spain	11	5	16
1	Slovakia	4 100	190	4 290
20	Sweden	2 506	116	2 622
2	Switzerland	400	115	515
45	Turkey	700	270	970
40	United Kingdom	28 000	900	28 900
294		133 461	11 101	144 562
	Americas			
180<	Brazil	1 500	0	1 500
23	Canada	1 853	144	1 997
4	Chile	200	0	200
1	Ecuador	35	0	35
55	Mexico	18 000	150	18 150
17	USA	55 500	1 500	57 000
280		77 088	1 794	78 882
	Africa			
3	Morocco	40	20	60
9	South Africa	500	23	523
12		540	43	583
	Asia			
1	China	0	12	12
4	Hong Kong	128	132	260
25	Indonesia	475	25	500
2	India	60	0	60
43	Japan	18 900	643	19 543
15	Malaysia	1 100	20	1 120
1	Philippines	15	0	15
18	Singapore	1 100	170	1 270
44	South Korea	11 500	450	11 950
1	Sri Lanka	6	0	6
1	Taiwan	0	101	101
8	Thailand	595	5	600
165		33 879	1 558	35 437
	Australasia			
15	Australia	1 300	60	1 360
1	New Zealand	20	0	20
16		1 320	60	1 380
767	Total world-wide factoring volumes	246 288	14 556	260 844

* Estimated as at December 1993.
< Est. 1992 FCI.
Source: Factors Chain International.

Table 12.2 International factoring growth 1980–1993

	1980	1981	1982	1983	1984	1985	1986	1987	1988	1989	1990	1991	1992	1993
World	100	103	103	113	120	143	175	235	270	319	410	448	444	439
		3%	0%	10%	6%	19%	22%	34%	15%	18%	29%	9%	-1%	-1%
FCI	100	100	96	106	108	159	207	305	352	448	550	581	593	617
		0%	-4%	10%	2%	47%	30%	47%	15%	27%	23%	6%	2%	4%
Austria	100	138	131	129	132	133	138	153	166	176	196	221	240	240
		38%	-5%	-2%	2%	1%	4%	11%	8%	6%	11%	13%	9%	0%
Belgium	100	95	122	160	201	229	274	279	324	401	502	558	587	675
		-5%	28%	31%	26%	14%	20%	2%	16%	24%	25%	11%	5%	15%
Canada	100	105	102	91	95	120	137	144	138	185	185	189	183	203
		5%	-3%	-11%	4%	26%	14%	5%	-4%	34%	0%	2%	-3%	11%
Denmark	100	95	126	140	170	159	163	166	205	286	373	500	532	548
		-5%	33%	11%	21%	-6%	3%	2%	23%	40%	30%	34%	6%	3%
Finland	100	144	185	230	273	316	305	320	372	399	348	197	202	218
		44%	28%	24%	19%	16%	-3%	5%	16%	7%	-13%	-43%	3%	8%
France	100	147	195	211	240	248	294	379	480	585	690	767	888	915
		47%	33%	8%	14%	3%	19%	29%	27%	22%	18%	11%	16%	3%
Germany	100	115	110	115	120	133	161	184	177	191	235	245	286	295
		15%	-4%	5%	4%	11%	21%	14%	-4%	8%	23%	4%	17%	3%
Italy	100	207	396	600	958	1475	1935	2920	4076	5890	7424	7860	8100	7452
		107%	91%	52%	60%	54%	31%	51%	40%	45%	26%	6%	3%	-8%
Japan	100	112	103	202	213	172	180	173	258	259	404	435	455	441
		12%	-8%	96%	5%	-19%	5%	-4%	49%	0%	56%	8%	5%	-3%
Mexico	n/a	n/a	n/a	n/a	n/a	n/a	n/a	100	235	1235	2313	6015	7415	6006
									135%	426%	87%	160%	23%	-19%
Netherlands	100	105	116	155	188	228	262	278	346	372	482	534	490	598
		5%	10%	34%	21%	21%	15%	6%	24%	8%	30%	11%	-8%	22%
Norway	100	127	145	160	192	211	253	326	264	208	214	217	201	221
		27%	14%	10%	20%	10%	20%	29%	-19%	-21%	3%	1%	-7%	10%
South Korea	n/a	n/a	n/a	n/a	100	317	394	817	1055	1870	3086	4597	8136	8868
						217%	24%	107%	29%	77%	65%	49%	77%	9%
Spain	n/a	n/a	n/a	n/a	100	119	291	425	570	750	931	1431	1469	2115
						19%	145%	46%	34%	32%	24%	54%	3%	44%
Sweden	100	109	124	128	120	121	103	86	94	81	107	88	81	75
		9%	14%	3%	-6%	1%	-15%	-17%	9%	-14%	32%	-18%	-8%	-7%
UK	100	104	120	152	196	255	313	395	522	643	762	750	785	965
		4%	15%	27%	29%	30%	23%	26%	32%	23%	19%	-2%	5%	23%
USA	100	108	106	117	132	132	141	157	160	165	173	180	187	200
		8%	-2%	10%	13%	0%	7%	11%	2%	3%	5%	4%	4%	7%

Base = 1980 in $ for World and FCI.
Base = 1980 in local currency except for Mexico and South Korea ($).
Source: Factors Chain International.

Away from the developed world, countries developing their economic and social structures are beginning to take advantage of the facilities. South America, previously the subject of so many banking sector write-offs, are returning with a vengeance as their economies begin to develop once more. Equally as the former Eastern Bloc begins to develop away from its historic roots, so the financial systems are developing sufficiently to enable factoring to commence.

The factoring concept has also recently touched previously difficult markets. China is one of the most recent countries to join the world-wide marketplace, with the Bank of China setting up a factoring subsidiary to assist with Chinese exports. At the time of writing, negotiations with parties in India and Vietnam are currently under way with a view to establishing factoring companies within these countries.

THE PROMOTION OF INTERNATIONAL TRADE AND FACTORING

The world-wide factoring market is principally dominated by two international chains, which offer support for the exporting company and provide a framework of collaboration between factoring companies within different countries. They are:

- The International Factors Group
- Factors Chain International.

The IF group was the first group of associated factoring companies to join together to form an informal group of collaborating factoring companies. In 1968, Factors Chain International was established and set up as an umbrella organisation for the independent factoring companies around the world.

Typically using a domestic factoring company as the intermediary, factoring clients can use the respective chains to allow access to export facilities world-wide. The associated member then provides the necessary local skills to provide effective credit management and credit assessment. By using a member of one of the chains, a domestic client can have their exports chased and protected as if they had their own local presence.

FACTORING AS PART OF A GLOBAL CORPORATE STRATEGY

For a number of companies, factoring has been used as an important strategic tool to ease the penetration of export markets on a global basis. Using their domestic factor as the co-ordinator, those companies trading globally can have automatic access to credit management and control activities across the world's developed economies. This gives the global company the opportunity to expand their export sales whilst ensuring efficient credit control and protection against bad debts.

Global case study

Shimano Industrial Co. Ltd, Japan

Shimano Industrial Co. Ltd's long history began in 1921 as the Shimano Iron Works, manufacturers of free wheels. Later, in 1951, the company merged with the Shimano Bicycle Co. Ltd to form the basis of the substantial producer of bicycle components, fishing tackle and 'cold forged' products for the automobile industry and other related sectors. Shimano has an innovative product range – a range now used widely and internationally by cyclists and sports fishers in many parts of the world.

Shimano has been trading internationally since 1931 and over a quarter of a century ago it established a presence in the USA to sell bicycle components and fishing tackle directly to the American market. Since then, cross-border operations have become a significant part of Shimano's overall growth strategy. Subsidiaries now exist in Europe, Canada and Singapore and affiliates have been formed in Australia, Thailand and the Republic of Korea. In addition an equity interest has been taken in an Italian manufacturer, and the company is working to expand its overseas production capabilities by adding a new factory in South East Asia in order to meet growing demand for their products from outside Japan.

Shimano now employs nearly 1000 people and enjoys world-wide sales of approximately $1bn per annum. It's a thriving business, increasingly export oriented, seeking to exploit fresh market opportunities wherever they arise.

It was that latter aspect which led the company to recognise the benefits available to them through an export factoring agreement. Shimano first signed a factoring contract in 1984 in order to obtain full credit protection against losses which were arising in connection with exports to Denmark. The facility initially covered sales volumes of approximately $1.3m per annum, but that has subsequently grown both in size and diversity, with credit-protected sales in 1993 approaching $20m in several countries.

Shimano feels that a considerable element in their success overseas has been the result of their decision to become involved in international factoring.

> It's an inexpensive and efficient way for a business to take advantage of export opportunities and to save time, staff resources, costs and difficulties. We have an improved predictable cash flow and a financial facility which grows in line with our sales. We have reduced the risk of bad debts and achieved full credit cover on the ultimate importers of our products. That, in turn, has led to reduced administrative overheads, savings on accounting equipment, machinery, stationery and office space – reduced overheads which otherwise would have been incurred in sales ledger work, credit investigation, and debt collection. We can make more cost effective use of our management time and expertise, all of which improves our competitiveness and enhances our own trading prospects.

Shimano has recognised that size and product reputation alone do not necessarily overcome some of the problems encountered in cross-border trade. The benefits of an export factoring agreement using the world-wide FCI network are an integral part of the company's overseas success and have considerably helped Shimano to increase its international competitiveness.

Source: adapted from an FCI case study within 'The International Factoring Report', 1993, p.12.

THE EASTERN BLOC

Radical changes have been seen within the eastern bloc in recent years, with the removal of communist rule and the development towards capitalism in its place. With the growing strains of development, Hungary, the Czech Republic and Slovakia have all entered the factoring arena in recent years.

Their initial entry into the factoring arena was to enable exports, the lifeblood of economic growth, to be effectively facilitated. Equally, as their own domestic banking and economic systems have developed, so the use of domestic factoring facilities has recently been launched. Although recent in their inception, Hungary now has six factoring companies, and the Czech Republic and Slovakia, three (Table 12.3).

Table 12.3 Development of factoring facilities within the eastern bloc ($m)

	Czechoslovakia			Hungary		
	1990	1992	1993*	1990	1992	1993
Domestic factoring business	0	0	98	0	0	10
Export factoring business	135	84	93	130	100	50
Totals	135	84	191	130	100	50

*Czech Republic and Slovakia combined.
Source: FCI reports, 1990, 1992 and statistics 1993.

Case study – Eastern Bloc

Porcela Plus, Czech Republic

Bohemian porcelain is indisputably one of the most traditional Czech products. Admired and desired since its appearance in the late seventeenth century, this fine china has long been exported. The earliest exports around 1800 were coffee sets from the works in Slakov, in the West Bohemian region noted for quality kaolin.

The more recent history of Bohemian porcelain exports date from the second half of the 1940s, when all export activities were under one state-owned foreign trade corporation, Ceskoslovenská Keramika. In 1991, when the economic and political situation changed, individual manufacturers or groups of manufacturers took over those exports.

That was an initial step in the founding of Porcela Plus, which now includes all the manufacturers of household and decorative china that were once part of the Karlovarksy Porcelán Sector Corporation. Subsequently, these manufacturers and their export entity, Porcela Plus, have gone through the process of privatisation and formed individual companies to co-operate among themselves. Currently the household and decorative china handled by Porcela Plus accounts for more than 80% of the Czech Republic's total exports in this field.

As the successor of Ceskoslovenská Keramika, Porcela Plus continues to supply its products not only to countries such as Austria, Italy and the Netherlands that have no significant porcelain industries of their own, but also to countries such as France, Germany and Great Britain competing head-on with their respective top brands. They also have well-established contacts with Australia, Belgium, Canada, Ireland, Portugal, Spain, Switzerland, the Scandinavian countries, South Africa, the USA and others.

Using an export factoring facility, the company's export factor deals with some 140 debtors in fourteen countries. In every case, use is made of the two-factor system using correspondent members of Factors Chain International within the importing country.

Porcela Plus has continued the seven factoring contracts of its predecessor for the export of Bohemian porcelain. The initial contract was made with a Swedish factor in 1981, when export factoring was mainly needed to provide reliable credit cover on those purchasing from the exporters. The ceramics/china industry is one in which open account terms are generally required. Factoring provides a reduction in risk exposure and protection against bad debts.

The turnover achieved through export factoring increased from $5.5m in 1991 to over $8m in 1992, and continues to rise.

Mr R. Kvet, the managing director of Porcela Plus, summarises his views of export factoring:

> It is an efficient way to ensure full credit cover on our buyers abroad with one agreement with a single factoring company that covers fourteen countries under the same conditions. At the same time, our company saves time and staff resources, and eliminates the various difficulties inherent in cross-border trade with different countries. Now the factor takes care of the administration of our foreign receivables.

Source: adapted from an FCI case study within 'The International Factoring Report', 1993, p.10.

FACTORING AND DEVELOPING COUNTRIES

With so much economic and social change currently happening throughout the world's economies, new opportunities for the world-wide factoring industry are developing. As the former USSR breaks into individual states as part of its development towards a capitalist system, so the need for hard currency to aid internal development has become the focus of respective governmental policies. Export-led growth, the tenet of classic economic growth theory, will be crucial to generating hard currency.

With the internal banking and financial systems in their very early stages of development, the variety of services available continue to be very limited. As a result, the member states are looking towards the western banking system for assistance. By joining in the world-wide chains of factoring companies on a micro level, the finance houses can provide assistance to the ambitious small business in the developing states by providing the framework to ease the process of exporting, whilst at the same time reducing the inherent risks contained within export credit. At the same time they will play a part in satisfying the governmental macroeconomic goal of export-led growth.

Mr Jeroen Kohnstamm, Secretary General of FCI, recently confirmed that many finance professionals within the URS states are taking a serious view of factoring, with a number of delegates from the URS having attended a recent conference examining the viability of establishing factoring organisations within their respective member states.

FACTORING AND DIFFICULT MARKETS

As the world economy continues to develop, many countries previously regarded as difficult markets are now emerging as countries open for business. Political, economic and social difficulties have been reduced enabling the benefits of trade to be seen by all concerned.

However, there remain a number of countries whose political and economic positions continue to engender instability, making them very difficult markets in which to offer open terms other than irrevocable confirmed letters of credit. Most African states and parts of the Middle East remain hotspots which the factoring market is unable to accommodate.

Summary

The underlying growth in the provision of factoring and invoice discounting facilities has been notable over the past 10 years, despite a recent lull in activity. The market continues to develop world-wide, with the majority of developed countries now having factoring companies, recognising the profit opportunities that can be realised through supporting the export development of their respective countries.

The emphasis on export-led growth as a political and economic expedient has equally developed factoring opportunities within previously difficult markets, with the changes within the political and economic structure of the world economy only helping to develop the marketplace further.

NOTES

1   Interpolating world-wide statistics issued from Factors Chain International (FCI).

Chapter 13

Export factoring

In this chapter we help the reader identify whether this service would be useful for her or his particular business or clients. We also take a broader view on the reasons for the lack of market penetration for what we feel is a very valuable service and possible ways forward. As factoring and invoice discounting are not used to finance capital goods, we have not covered this aspect of UK exports. We also look at the role government has played in supporting the UK exporter. Contributions from Mr Robin Ebers, Deputy Director-General of the Institute of Export, have been particularly helpful.

MARKET OVERVIEW

The UK's exports amount to around £105 billion[1] per annum, of which we estimate £70 billion are made up of consumables or potentially 'factorable' goods and services. Consumer goods or consumables in factoring terms can be anything from standard engineering components to goods sold to retailers, e.g. clothing, PCs, microwave ovens and equipment and machinery up to a unit value of say £5000 to £10 000. The Institute of Export reckon there are between 40 000 and 60 000 exporters in the UK.

The government has stated that it is keen to promote exports as a means of boosting economic recovery, however, financial support from the High Street banks is limited at present to Midland Bank's Midfes scheme and Barclays' Tradeline. We were advised by an industry expert that the volume of sales supported by these two schemes is around £1 billion. Managers from other clearing banks maintain that the bank overdraft is the finance vehicle often used for export sales.

'The Government provides a whole range of different services for companies wishing to start out in export, it has plenty of advice but there is no funding available. It is against the principals of GATT for the Government to subsidise exporters.' Robin Ebers of the Institute of Export sums up the situation for exporters.

The decrease in support for UK exports of consumable items has been significant over the last fifteen years and is primarily linked to the fortunes of our state insurer ECGD (Export Credits Guarantee Department). The role of ECGD, established in 1919, was to promote UK exports by providing credit insurance, thus ensuring security of payment and the granting of associated finance during the credit period. In the halcyon days of 'The Comprehensive Bankers Guarantee' exporters could obtain finance from their bank at 5/8ths over bank base rate! The banks were happy to lend at these fine margins as they had a guarantee from ECGD for 100% reimbursement of any losses. Unfortunately for the exporter the scheme was withdrawn due to fraud and to the heavy losses sustained by ECGD as a result of poor maintenance of the policy conditions by the exporter.

The UK export market has been subject to significant changes:

- 1985–87: withdrawal of the Comprehensive Bankers' Guarantee Scheme by ECGD;
- 1991: the privatisation of the Insurance Services Group arm of ECGD through NCM (Nederlandsche Credietverzekering Maatschaappi NV) and the establishment of NCM Credit Insurance;
- 1990–93 phasing out and withdrawal of the short-term smaller exporter finance schemes by two of the big four banks. The reason for withdrawal was mainly fraud. One of the banks that did stay in the market was Barclays, 'We remained in the market to help customers... The way we managed our services was different to some other banks... Barclays branch managers are responsible locally for lending under our schemes so there is more hands on control. Our head office looks after the credit insurance side only.' So said Ian Stuttard of their International Trade Services Division.

EXPORTERS MUST OFFER CREDIT TERMS TO COMPETE

If exporters cannot grant their customers credit, they cannot compete on an equal basis with suppliers in the country of the customer and other competitors. Credit can only be offered if reserves or funding are available to maintain their cash flow over the credit period.

With this background, export factoring volumes in the UK have grown over the last five years, reaching around £500 million[2] in 1993. Market penetration is, according to our estimates, less than 1%. Of the 60 or so factoring and invoice discounting companies, around 12 offer export facilities. These are mainly from the larger factors. Capital investment in communications systems, overseas networks, appropriately trained personnel are needed to provide export factoring services. Thus competition in the market is largely limited to bank-owned factors, who have the systems to handle the risks associated with exports.

EXPORT FACTORING – HOW IT WORKS

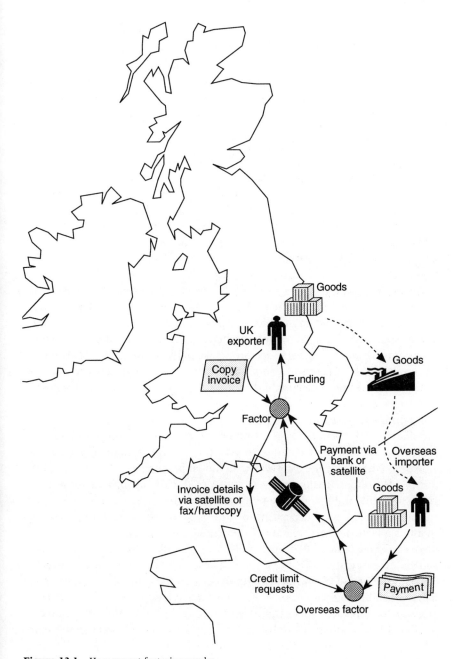

Figure 13.1   How export factoring works

The mechanisms

The exporter signs a factoring agreement with the export factor based in the UK. Through the agreement, all export invoices are assigned to the factor.

The factor reassigns the debts to its overseas correspondent(s) in the country of the debtor.

Under some agreements whereby the factors provide bad debt protection, the overseas factor will investigate the credit standing of the buyer(s), and establish approved credit lines. This enables the exporter to sell goods and services on open account terms while maintaining security of payment (a useful alternative to payment by letters of credit in markets where political risks are insignificant).

As sales take place and goods or services are despatched in accordance with the sales contract the exporter sends copy invoices to the UK-based factor who transmits details to the overseas factor who will then handle collections. The UK factor will advance funds as per the factoring agreement.

The overseas factor will remit the funds collected. In the event of non-payment due to risks covered by the bad debt protection, the overseas factor will remit funds. Any legal charges involved in pursuing the debts are generally met by the overseas factor in a full factoring service. See Figure 13.1 for a schematic of export factoring.

An exporter can gain great benefit from using an export factor who is a member of a factoring chain or has correspondents who will assist with credit assessment and receivables chasing in the country of the customer. Some bank-owned factors are linked to 'chains', i. e. groups of overseas correspondents, however, others operate collections from the UK. Lombard Natwest and Alex Lawrie Factors have collections departments in the UK. Kellock can arrange collection either from the UK or though correspondents in selected countries.

Having a representative in the customer's country can give advantages, familiarity with the language, awareness of customs, payment excuses and local risks enables the UK factor to give the exporter a value-added service. However, when selecting a service it should be borne in mind that two sets of overheads are potentially involved, those of the UK factor and those of its correspondent, and this may be reflected in the cost of the facility.

The UK factor will, depending on the type of export factoring arrangement, apply to its correspondents for credit limit approvals on its clients' prospective customers. Bad debt protection of up to 100% of invoice values can be given against two principal risks, debtor insolvency and protracted default. The period of protracted default prior to the coming into force of the factor's liability can vary from 90 days past due date upwards. Longer periods are usually stipulated for certain 'slow' markets such as Italy. Protection is restricted to the areas of insolvency and payment default because these are where the factor is most expert.

It should be noted that political risks are not covered by factors thus their cover is suitable in markets where these risks are minimal; the EU, Scandinavia, North America, Australia, New Zealand and some Asian markets. Alternatively, the exporter's own credit insurance policy can be assigned to the UK factor or discounter and credit limits be applied for as normal. For smaller exporters, factors such as Alex Lawrie have their own export credit insurance policy through which they can obtain cover. It is recommended that companies trading with politically 'high risk' markets should seek cover from traditional credit insurers.

When goods have been shipped the exporter copies invoices to the UK factor in the usual way, sometimes appending proof of shipment. The factor will finance as agreed and transmit the exporters' invoice details and/or copy invoices to its correspondent in the county of the customer. Members of the largest chain, FCI (Factors Chain International), joined the EDIFACT system in May 1994, through which they can send invoice information electronically. The other chains in existence in 1994 are the Heller chain and the International Factors Group.

The correspondent will collect the monies due and remit them to the UK factor, or pay over sums in accordance with its bad debt protection

BENEFITS OF EXPORT FACTORING

Faster collections

Robin Ebers comments on how factors can help exporters:

> When companies are finding that debts are slipping and their average outstandings are growing to 90 plus days, they then will have a cash flow problem. Providing they don't have a cash flow crisis it is good for factors to then look into that problem and to demonstrate how they can help them.

Whether the factor collects from the UK or via an overseas correspondent, there is likely to be a reduction in the time it takes the client to pay. It is understandable that firm, professional collection procedures would contribute to a faster inflow of payments. Mark Runiewicz, trade finance consultant at the Bank Relationship Consultancy, puts a figure on this and gives a useful example:

> Experience shows that companies using factors obtain payment faster than when traditional payment methods are used... A company with a turnover of £2m can expect to save about £25 000 in costs or 1.25% of turnover in a year. Company A exports 90% of its £2m turnover... The company receives payments on average within 60 days from the date of despatch for which it requires working capital of £300 000. The company had an overdraft facility of £50 000 and funded the balance of its

working capital need from reserves, causing pressure on its liquidity. The company's bank would not increase the overdraft because of the large proportion of overseas debts...the company was granted a factoring facility of 85% of its debtor book with a limit of £240 000. The factor provided finance and a debt collection service in the buyer's country... debtor days were reduced from 60 to 45, reducing interest charges and increasing working capital.

Efficiency – saving time and bank charges

Transmission of funds can be by satellite, as in the case of the International Factors Group. As various correspondents collect funds on behalf of other group members the receivables are netted off and only extra amounts are forwarded to the home-based factor. Cost and time savings over normal bank transmission of funds can be significant, e.g. average charge for an international transfer is £15, 12 transfers per year per customer equals £180, for 10 customers equals £1800. Robin Ebers told us that many UK exporters are also sceptical of the delays in the banks' transferring monies from overseas.

The exporter's life is also made easier by being able to liaise with one UK based factor rather than banks overseas to obtain payment.

Financing credit periods

It should be remembered that the exporter must compete with indigenous suppliers and therefore has to generally support a longer period of credit than is required for home sales. Sales terms of up to 90 days are commonly financed with 120 days generally the maximum length of credit supported by a factor or discounter. Mr. Ebers' view: 'The company can draw down how much it wants...it can draw down up to 80%, as much as it requires which means it doesn't have to pay interest on that total sum.'

Foreign currency risk reduction and accounting

For a company selling in foreign currency with the majority of its cost of sales in sterling, conversion of sales proceeds to sterling is necessary. Waiting for 90 days or more for receipt of funds could mean adverse changes in exchange rates. Companies which factor can ask for their prepayment of say 70% of invoice value in sterling on the day the factor receives a copy of the currency invoice, thus restricting the risk of currency fluctuation to two or three days from raising of the sales invoice. In some cases factors will make available in sterling 100% of the foreign currency invoice, taking their 30% retention from the client's domestic ledger, thus enabling the client to close out completely its foreign exchange risk. At the time of writing our country does not participate in the ERM. Should we return to the mechanism then this will be less of a benefit as exchange rate movements are restricted. See Figures 13.2 and 13.3 for FX risk reduction schematics.

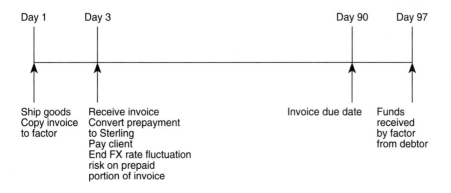

Figure 13.2 Foreign exchange rate fluctuation risk reduction

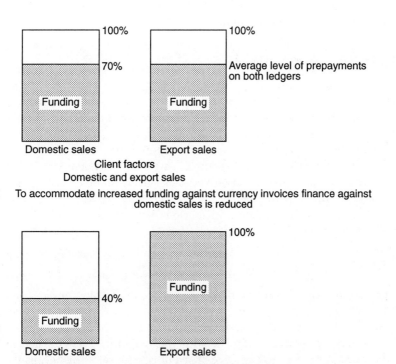

Figure 13.3 How the export factor and discounter are able to give 100% prepayment against foreign currency invoices

Factors offering export services can generally provide accounting in most major currencies and remit funds to clients in sterling thus obviating the need for smaller clients to invest in a multi-currency accounting package. Buyers will often prefer to pay in local currency or US dollars forcing UK businesses to quote and invoice accordingly. These benefits are recognised by Robin Ebers of the Institute of Export:

> The factoring process does help exporters on the exchange rate because the factor will pay the exporter in sterling...the factor will then take that risk.

Language

The correspondent can arrange collection in the language of the debtor and deal with any problems arising. It can be argued that so too can the factors' bilingual collection teams be based in the UK. The foreign language skills of most businesspeople are no doubt improving but one has to be a very proficient speaker to overcome delaying tactics and just how many languages would one need to speak to control one ledger?

Reducing clients' overheads

Clients can avoid employing full time credit management staff with foreign language skills. The management trend of the 90s of out sourcing non-core business activities provides extra endorsement for directors to place collections and credit control in the hands of external experts. Many factors provide on-line management systems to clients. The FacFlow facility from Lombard NatWest is a typical example – a PC-based system which provides the exporter with information on the sales ledger through a screen in his or her own office. As with other systems it shows the amount of finance available from the factoring facility, the previous day's payments and a list of outstanding invoices.

Example

One user of export factoring is Ally Capellino, the fashion design company. The company turns over in excess of £1 million and sells to clients in Denmark, Japan, Greece, Singapore, Taiwan, Italy, USA, France and Belgium. The fashion industry is seasonal with the majority of sales made in the Spring and Autumn. With finance linked directly to sales this means there is no cash flow problem during the credit period.

Jonathan Platt, director, explained his reasons for using a factoring facility were not only to access suitable finance but to better manage the language barrier and the various trading customs. This leaves the directors free to do what they are best at.

Factoring in the EU

Italy is a prime example of how factoring can penetrate a market – with a population similar in size to that of the UK, factoring volume amounts to £40 billion per annum, compared to the UK's £16 billion in 1992. See Chapter 12 for more details.

Fears of clients, however unfounded, that their customers will think they are in difficulty may be overcome by logical examination of the benefits of factoring to the debtors: local payment in their own currency, and talking in their own language to a representative in their own country.

WEAKNESSES

Sales to debtors in countries outside the OECD cannot generally be financed, there are occasional exceptions to this, however, the factor can in most cases arrange traditional 'bank collection' services through its parent.

Finance for pre-shipment manufacturing periods is not available as is funding against Letters of Credit. Minimum turnover of sales tends to be higher than that required for domestic products at around £50 000 to £100 000 per market for factoring and around £2 000 000 total for export invoice discounting. Those factors collecting overseas debts from the UK may consider lower turnovers per market. Capital and semi-capital goods (e.g. big construction and shipbuilding plant, trucks etc.) are not suitable for invoice discounting and factoring and maximum allowable credit periods are often set at around 90 days by the factors.

THE FAILURE OF MARKETING?

Consider the benefits of export factoring, coupled with the general absence of any similar 'value-added' bank schemes and one would expect a lot of UK exporters to take advantage of them. This, however, is not the case.

One reason for the lack of take-up is in our view that the factors themselves have been ambivalent in the running and marketing of these services. From 1980 domestic factoring and invoice discounting grew from £1 billion to £13 billion in 1990. What need had they of trying to promote export factoring when growth based on existing domestic services was sufficient to meet shareholders' demands? Export services appear to have developed in response to the needs of a few domestic clients who required funding and administration for their growing sales ledgers.

The major factoring houses may be accused of complacency. Being bank-owned they typically derived the majority of their new business from their parent. This flow of new business faltered during 1990 and 1991 due to the recession. New business taken on as a result of bank introductions fell with numbers of existing clients suffering reduced turnover and failure. External forces prompted some factors into developing new services – they at last viewed exporters as a viable market. Now in 1994 the flow of clients from the parent banks has returned and it appears that the worst of the recession is over. Now that it is 'business as usual' again it remains to be seen whether the factors will continue in a significant way to develop and promote services for exporters.

Starting from a low base of approximately £500 million of sales factored in 1993 it will be hard work for factors to convince potential users of the merits of their services. As the reader will appreciate from Chapter 16, most business services, such as factoring, are purchased as a result of positive advice from a respected influencer of opinion. Among these we would number accountants, export organisations, bank managers, credit insurance brokers, the DTI and the users themselves. Forging relationships with such influencers will help market penetration, but this will take the factors time, investment and vision to achieve. Meanwhile we can expect disappointingly small volumes.

Intra-bank communications could be strengthened, with the factor reminding appropriate managers of their services and the benefits for clients. Branch bank managers have around 200 banking products in their portfolio, export factoring is just one of them.

Reorganisation of the banks has meant that export accounts are often handled by dedicated service offices and not the small business centres with whom the factoring salespeople maintain contact. We are unaware of any factors which require salespeople to have experience in some form or another of exporting apart from the occasional example of export operations managers being moved into export sales. These are few and far between. It is common practice for salespeople to call on in-house export operations managers to be present at meetings with potential export clients to handle detailed queries.

EXPORT FACTORING AND THE PROFESSIONAL ADVISOR

As discussed in Chapter 16, the accountant in particular is a key figure in influencing the business decisions of small companies. In the specialised area of exporting they almost certainly need training. Ebers comments:

> the accountant is somebody who is pretty weighed down in a small business anyhow, looking at the financial standing, cash flow and working capital, but most know little about the impact of export, most know nothing about the advantages of multi currency financing, most shiver at the thought of taking out forward cover on foreign debts...and many don't know anything about documentary credits.

We feel that the low market penetration of these services is due to:

1. lack of training in the issues facing exporters among key advisors to small businesses, i.e. accountants and bank managers – we can put this down to work loads and to difficulties for these generalists to acquire more and more 'niche' market skills;
2. a general lack of successful promotion of export services and their benefits.

IS EXPORT FACTORING SUITABLE FOR YOUR COMPANY?

The following list of questions is designed to help you decide whether export factoring could benefit your company. If you meet the basic criteria below continue to answer the questions following.

Basic criteria

- Is your product or service factorable?
- Are you forecasting exports of £200 000 plus per annum to developed countries, on credit terms of up to 120 days? If the answers to these are yes please continue.[3]

Funding

- If your customers could pay on open account terms instead of Letters of Credit, could you sell more? And if so how will you fund the credit period and deal with the risk on non-payment and debtor insolvency?
- Do you need working capital to fund your export sales?
- Do you turn away new business due to lack of working capital?
- If you had extra working capital to pay suppliers earlier could you benefit from prompt payment discounts?

Collections

- Are you satisfied with your/your staff's collection performance?
- Could your/their time be spent more productively on other areas of the business?
- If sales increase will you/your staff be able to manage the extra collection work?

Sundry costs

- What are the costs of chasing overseas debts, phone, fax and mail?
- Have you used a solicitor? If so what were the costs?
- How much do you spend on bank charges relating to international fund transfers?

Credit management

- Do you have credit insurance?
- If no, what is the value of bad debts suffered?
- If no, are your systems for credit checking customers sufficient?

Savings in many of the above cost areas can be made by using factoring. Ask the factor how they can help in each area and weigh up the commercial benefits to your company. Seek professional advice before entering an agreement.

Summary

Export factoring could help a lot more businesses compete overseas. It has more intrinsic benefits than its domestic counterpart and yet is usually overlooked. It deserves recognition. Government, via the DTI, could help exporters and factors by acknowledging the value of the services on offer, not only as a means of raising finance but also of effectively managing the commercial risks of cross-border trading.

As long as the major factors are being fed most of their new clients by the clearing banks they are unlikely to use their considerable marketing budgets to promote this service. Possibly with the entry of the larger independents into the market and the nurturing of non-bank 'influencers of opinion' such as accountants, business consultants and export organisations, there will be significant market penetration.

Whichever factor is first to successfully communicate the benefits of its services to influencers of business opinion and to exporters themselves will be set to achieve significant penetration in this huge, untapped market.

Table 13.1 Export services

Finance	Full service factoring up to 80%	Recourse factoring up to 80%	Invoice discounting up to 80%
Credit checking of buyers	Yes	Yes, with some facilities	Yes, with some facilities
Bad debt protection	Yes, by the factoring chain	usually client's own credit insurance	usually credit cover is a requirement
Collection of accounts receivable	Yes	Yes	No
Accounts receivable book-keeping and statements	Yes	Yes	No

Table 13.2 Comparison between non-recourse factoring and credit insurance

Small businesses need	Factors provide	Credit insurers provide
Cover against insolvency	Yes	Yes
Cover against protracted default	Yes	Yes
Political risks, war, moratoria on external debt	No	Yes
Prompt payment on proof of debtor insolvency	Yes	Yes
Prompt payment against political risk claims	Not applicable	No, can be 18 or 24 months' waiting period
Credit control and debt chasing	Yes	No
Prompt credit limit decisions	Sometimes	Generally
Approved limits for required amount	Sometimes	Likely – able to underwrite higher limits
Pre-shipment cover	No	Sometimes on period and type of goods

Credit insurers such as NCM have vast databases of overseas buyers. NCM has for many years provided domestic and credit insurance to Dutch exporters and now also benefits from the experience of the former ISG* team of underwriters plus the ISG automatic credit limit system. It was the boast of ISG in 1990 that 80% of credit limit decisions were advised within 24 hours.

We should also mention TI as another major UK-based export and domestic credit insurer, and the main competitor to ECGD.

*ISG, Insurance Services Group, was part of ECGD until 1991.

NOTES

1 Central Statistical Office, total 1993, excluding oil, ships, aircraft, precious stones and silver.
2 The ABF&D members do not keep separate statistics for import and export factoring. Both services are classified as international factoring. Total international factoring for ABF&D members for 1993 was £759 million.
3 If you do not meet the basic criteria it is still worth approaching a factoring broker who can advise you of any new facilities on the market. (This service should be provided free of charge.)

Chapter 14

Import factoring

The UK is a net importer of goods with £123 billion of goods excluding oil and erratics coming into the UK during 1993. Of this amount we estimate that around £75 billion were consumables (or items which are individually priced at under £5000 to £10 000). We have isolated the total of consumables to indicate the total potential size of the market for import factoring. Large value, or capital goods such as plant and machinery are not suitable for factoring.

This chapter may be of particular interest to overseas-based financial advisors and companies who are involved with exports of consumable goods to the UK. UK sales agents may also wish to consider import factoring as one way for their principals to secure payments for sales to the UK and to access funding.

We look at three types of import factoring. Two are designed to facilitate cash flow and administration for exporters, with and without the involvement of a factor in the country of the client. The third type is designed to help the UK company finance imports.

MARKET OVERVIEW

The UK has suffered recession for the last four or five years and many company failures will have caused losses for some overseas suppliers. We also suffer from a culture of slow payment.

Note also the failure of strong lobbying efforts by the Federation of Small Businesses, in particular, to introduce legislation for the levying of statutory interest on late payments in the UK.

Given that we import enormous volumes each year and that UK companies are among some of the worst payers in Europe, one would think that import factoring would be widely used.

Figures from the Association of British Factors and Discounters on the volume of import factoring carried out by its members are not recorded suggesting its lack of importance. They are instead included with the statistics for export factoring. Nevertheless most of the larger factors provide import factoring services. One of the leading factors, Alex Lawrie, quotes 5% of their total turnover being accounted for by import and export services.

PAYMENT OF IMPORTS

Imports are paid for in a number of ways. Those commonly used are letter of credit, open account and collection (bill of exchange presented for acceptance along with shipping documents).

Letter of credit

Opening a letter of credit (L/C) in favour of an overseas supplier takes time and will in many cases use a portion of a customer's credit line with its bank, effectively tying it up from the date of issue of the L/C to debiting of the customer's account. This can be anything from a few weeks to a few months. It involves the customer in a degree of processing, instructing the opening bank in writing, agreeing terms with the supplier and amending it if there are changes to the order or delivery arrangements.

The benefits of using this form of payment accrue mainly to the supplier in terms of security of payment, provided documentation is in order, and to access to finance as soon as documents are approved by the bank, by either getting paid under the L/C or discounting its proceeds. L/Cs are particularly useful when supplying to a customer in a country which is politically unstable or has shortage of foreign exchange. If the supplier arranges for an L/C in his or her favour, confirmed by a local reputable bank, these two risks are avoided.

In an increasingly competitive world, favourable terms of payment may be a decisive element in selecting a particular supplier. Why should a customer go the trouble of raising a letter of credit if equally acceptable goods can be obtained under simple open account terms?

Our view is that payment by L/C will continue to diminish in favour of open account trading for consumable goods.

Bill collection

This is less complicated for the buyer and seller and provides the seller with some security of payment. The typical scenario for use of bill collection would be an overseas supplier to a UK customer, goods are shipped in accordance with the underlying sales contract. Goods arrive in the UK port. The original bills of lading are issued by the shipping company to the supplier at time of sailing. These are sent to the customer's bank in the UK via the international banking system along with a bill of exchange drawn on the customer for the agreed amount. The customer's bank will release the original shipping documents to the customer as soon as he or she accepts the bill of exchange. Essentially acceptance means signing the bill and agreeing to pay the bill amount on the date given thereon. The supplier presents the bill for payment on the due date. The supplier benefits from the security of retaining the documents of title to the goods until the customer has shown his or her uncon-ditional agreement to pay for them at a specified date.

Open account

This is where buyer and seller arrange payment directly between themselves without the security (or expense) of the above two methods. Payment is made as it is generally for normal domestic sales at say 45 days from despatch. Credit periods for imports and for exports tend to be longer to take into account the longer delivery time. Overseas suppliers must match or better credit terms granted by local suppliers.

As far as administration is concerned this is the easiest and cheapest route, payment against simple invoice. However the supplier is wide open to the risk of non-payment. As more businesses insist on paying by this method more suppliers will be at risk due to a variety of causes.

Cash in advance

As one of the major factors says, this is 'nice work if you can get it'.

IMPORT FACTORING

In the UK this is mainly limited to a collections and/or bad debt protection service, with the finance sometimes being provided by the bank or factor in the country of the exporter. However, there are some UK factors who will also give finance as well as the collections service.

In our view it can be an effective way for exporters to the UK to obtain a professional collections service with the option of bad debt protection to give security of payment. Effort on the part of the customer in the UK is min-imised, in fact he or she is likely to find it easier to make payments to the UK-based factor rather than make international transfers. Dealing with a col-lector who is fluent in English may also have its advantages.

Import factoring – how it works

Direct import factoring

The factoring agreement is directly between the UK-based factor and the client overseas. This can often be arranged by post and telephone. Debts are thus assigned to the factor. Where bad debt protection is provided the factor will investigate the credit standing of the buyer(s) and establish credit lines.

As sales take place and goods are despatched in accordance with the sales contract, the exporter sends copy invoices to the factor. The factor will begin to chase and collect debts as agreed with the client.

As the funds are collected they are remitted to the client – some factors agree the minimum amount to be transferred to the client to save on transmission charges. In the event of non-payment where the cause relates to a risk covered under the bad debt protection element of the service, the UK factor will make good the shortfall to the client. Bad debt protection will cover maybe from 75% to 100% of the invoice value subject to the debt being approved by the factor. There can also be an excess.

Protecting against bad debts when dealing with the UK on open account makes good business sense – overseas firms should look closely at the relative costs and benefits of factoring as against credit insurance.

Variations

Funding from the UK factor   Some factors will provide funding as well as bad debt protection and collections. In this situation the factor may accept an assignment of the rights of the exporter's credit insurance policy rather than using its own bad debt protection service.

UK and non-UK sales can be factored   The best way to explain this is to give an example, an exporter in Argentina supplying the UK, Germany and France can assign invoices on all these sales to a UK-based factor. The factor will use its correspondents in Germany and France to undertake credit investigation, collection and possibly bad debt protection. The mechanisms for this would be along the lines of export factoring.

Indirect import factoring

The supplier or client will have an agreement with a factor in its country (the export factor), who will send invoices to the UK factor to collect. This service is a mirror image of export factoring using overseas correspondents. As with direct importing the UK-based non-recourse factor can offer bad debt protection. Credit approval requests will be routed through the local factor.

The mechanisms

The supplier or client will have an agreement with a factor in its country (the export factor) who will send invoices to the UK factor to collect. The UK factor will undertake credit assessment collections and bad debt protection as required.

Remittances, EDIFACT and satellite

When payments are received by the UK factor the client's account is credited. Funds will be remitted to the export factor (who may have financed the sale). Minimum transfer amounts can be established thereby avoiding charges on forwarding small sums. There are various ways for the factors to transmit funds.

Barclays Commercial Services, a member of the largest chain, Factors' Chain International (FCI), transfers funds by SWIFT. Associated charges are passed on to the export factor.

FCI joined EDIFACT on May 1st 1994. The acronym stands for Electronic Data Interchange For Administration, Commerce and Transport. It was developed by the UN to facilitate international trade and reduce paperwork. Membership of EDIFACT has given FCI pole position over its competitors The Heller Group and the International Factors Group. It is understood that the latter are now seeking membership of EDIFACT.

The use of EDIFACT obviates the need to mail copy invoices, or hard copy credit requests to the collecting factor.

True import factoring

Although some factors have tried to make this work, the underlying difficulty remains that at the time the client imports the goods, there is no enforceable debt from the importer to its customers which the factor can fund and use as security. Goods need to be delivered by the importer to end users before a debt is created. Without debt, factoring cannot work.

Previous attempts at providing this type of trade finance often resulted in the factor holding documents of title for imports that had been refused for contractual reasons by the end buyer in the UK.

Briefly, how this worked:

1. A trading company would win an order from a large high street retailer for goods sourced overseas.
2. The factor would support the issue of an L/C to enable the purchase of the goods or guarantee to the supplier payment from the eventual proceeds of the sale.
3. The end buyers would confirm that they would make payment for the goods via the factor.
4. Goods are shipped and the supplier paid. The trader receives them and delivers the same to the buyer. If accepted and paid for by the buyer, the factor is reimbursed for monies paid away to the overseas supplier. If the goods are rejected because they are poor quality, etc., the factor is left holding goods and an unenforceable invoice.

BENEFITS OF IMPORT FACTORING

Ease of administration

The UK factor can arrange collections after receipt of copy invoices as per domestic factoring. Using its skilled, obviously English-speaking, credit control personnel, aware of the excuses and delaying tactics and banking procedures, it can help secure the cash flow of the client. The factors can also send statements in English, saving the client time and money.

Factors are also familiar with the payment and administration procedures of the largest UK companies. These procedures often pose problems for small UK suppliers not to mention those from overseas battling with language and jargon. Administration costs are kept relatively low and will therefore not inflate the price of the goods.

Savings on bank transfer charges

International Factors Group makes use of a satellite to transmit credit approval requests. More importantly, through this system it is able to net off payments due from its members. This saves clients transfer charges and time delays, with monies being transferred to their account with the local factor almost at the touch of a button.

Security

Prompt chasing will highlight early on any problems with delivery or quality so that the client may resolve them with the buyer. Systematic collections are also more likely to prevent bad debts. An 'old debt is a cold debt'.

Non-recourse factors will of course offer bad debt protection giving the client the benefit of their experienced in-house, domestic underwriting team. The availability of funding from some UK factors is an added attraction especially as credit periods are longer. As with domestic and export factoring, funds would increase in line with approved sales.

Reduction in credit insurance costs

Collections carried out methodically and professionally can also be attractive to the client's credit insurer should there be one. The activities of the UK factor will effectively limit the risk of non-payment and therefore this may be reflected in a premium reduction for the client from the insurer.

Weaknesses of import factoring

It facilitates exports from other countries to the UK which, it could be said, is bad for our balance of payments. While indirect import factoring cost may be higher, there are two lots of overheads: for the factor in both the country of the exporter and the customer.

Political risks not covered

Factors can protect clients against commercial risks such as debtor insolvency and protracted payment default but they are not able to safeguard against political risks: shortage of foreign exchange, wars and embargoes, etc. As the

UK is politically stable these risks are negligible. The same also applies to most of the developed countries of the world. Where there is some doubt, it is recommended that payment is arranged by irrevocable letter of credit, confirmed in the country of the supplier or that appropriate insurance is taken out.

Funding

Many factors are not happy to fund clients based overseas for the following reason: due diligence or client assessment is time consuming and expensive by comparison with straightforward domestic factoring. As most losses incurred by factors originate from client failure or fraud many feel that funding a distant client is too risky.

However, at least one factor has taken a different approach and by use of an overseas field force and links through its parent bank's correspondents, mitigates its risk. One of the measures used to reduce client risk is to 'verify' each debt before funding. This is a simple process where debtors are asked to confirm that they have received the goods or services evidenced by the assigned invoices. We know of only one factor who has taken the initiative to put in a small bilingual field force and actively try to manage the client risk aspects of funding against imports.

THE FACTORS' VIEW

Factors like these services for several reasons. The reader has learned from other chapters that the major losses generally affecting factoring companies ironically lie with clients rather than debtors. Major and minor frauds by clients have been made against factors and discounters. Clients receive funds on the strength of copy invoices. Thus with import factoring, where no finance is provided to the client by the UK factor, risk is reduced and lies only with the debtors. But here the risk is manageable and factors have expertise. Underwriters are trained and experienced, a sensible premium can be built into the administration charge and sales to financially weak buyers need not be underwritten or 'approved'.

With indirect import the factor has not had to invest in marketing or selling to the client but can nevertheless generate fee income. Factors who do not provide import finance, and they are in the majority, will not of course gain any revenue associated with funding.

Greater use of the factors' major fixed overheads, collections and credit underwriting departments plus their attendant computer systems, makes economic sense.

Summary

Consider for a moment countries which export enormous volumes to the UK and EU. These would be prime markets for import factoring services – finance and/or collections. Where credit insurance is available and is used by the prospective client, the factor can either take an assignment over the exporter's policy and use this as extra security for providing finance or offer collection services only.

Nevertheless the bad debt protection element of import factoring can be just as cost effective as credit insurance; one factoring company we spoke to advised that their bad debt protection was cheaper than charges levied by COFACE, the French insurer, on the same debts.

What an opportunity: goods flooding into the UK year after year, the administrative problems and inconvenience of trading by letter of credit and bills of exchange and the collection and credit underwriting systems already in place.

Will one of the major factors, with potential overseas distribution through its parent bank's network of offices and correspondents, seize the initiative?

Chapter 15

Factoring and the bank manager

Here we look at the role played by bank managers as intermediaries between
the factor and potential new clients. Banks managers have been treated separately to other professional advisors in this book – they are not paid for
impartial advice regarding financing. Nevertheless, each small- and medium-
sized business has a bank account and managers are in a prime position to
influence the market.

OVERVIEW – CHANGE IN PUBLIC PERCEPTION

The public perception of banks and banking has undergone significant
change in the last twenty years. Bank managers, like other professionals,
were figures of reverence whose ability and impartiality were beyond question. Since that time we have seen the debacle of lending to the third world
hit profits of many banks including those in the UK. In more recent times we
have witnessed the losses made by the UK banks in lending on property and
to UK businesses in the 1980s. They are fallible.

The banks' subsequent change in lending policies to small- and medium-
sized enterprises (SMEs) at the beginning of the 90s caused protest from
businesses, especially smaller ones. During 1993 and 1994 the banks have
repaired their balance sheets and strengthened their capital base. There is
cash to lend but financing criteria must be amended to avoid the mistakes of
the past.

DOUBLE WHAMMY FOR SMALL BUSINESSES

The perceived role of the manager has changed in a generation from confi-
dante and business advisor of unquestioned probity to professional salesperson. One could argue that managers have always been salespeople but it is
only now with the pressures of recession that business customers are seeing

them in a truer light. The products are lending, insurance and other banking services but companies are now in no doubt that their bank is just another supplier of services. The recent trend towards 'relationship banking' has been viewed with scepticism by many customers.

One of the measures that has brought about this firmer approach is that banks have lost the non-interest earning lodgements. Thanks to the entry of building societies to the retail market with the interest paying current accounts there is no 'cheap money to be had'. As explained to us by one senior banker:

> Historically the benefit of these interest free lodgements provided a massive cross-subsidy to the Banks' lending, given the average return on these funds in a high inflation, high interest environment was significant. As we enter a period where expectations are of a low interest/low inflation environment and competition has all but eroded this subsidy there is a strong argument that the lending margins that now need to be charged must increase to make lending profitable for the banks.

Businesses in the 90s are dealt the double blow of a change in banking policy – payment of interest on more current accounts and other deposits – and the legacy of companies that failed during the recession leaving the banks with losses. Banks in the 80s were heavily reliant on the property sector, so when this collapsed, so did lending levels.

For the small business this means higher, albeit more realistic charges for borrowings and a more conservative attitude to lending from their main source of finance. In a market economy the removal of the hidden subsidy of 'cheap money' is to be welcomed but it is a bitter pill for the small business.

BANKS NEED SMALL BUSINESSES

Banks are facing much greater competition for other parts of their core business – notably services for large corporates on the one hand and the personal sector on the other. The role of the niche financiers is developing. It is not unusual for companies to approach factors, leasing organisations and international trade financiers without referring to their bank manager.

But the banks still need small business customers. According to the March 1994 report by Graham Bannock & Partners Ltd, entitled *The Future of Small Business Banking*, sponsored by National Westminster Bank, banks appear to generate more income from services provided to SMEs than from lending to them.

The report goes on to say in its executive summary:

> Yet it is essential that banks should have an incentive to lend to SMEs. That is why banks need to maintain or even increase their interest mar-

gins on their lending business. Tight control over the quality of loans is therefore of central importance for the future of banking – and especially of small business banking

Banks have tried to widen margins as interest rates have fallen but there have been well-publicised protests from customers and politicians to increases. We feel that the widening of margins to a realistic level will necessarily be a slow process. Given that they need customers from this growing and important sector of the economy but with reduced risk, how will they go about it?

THE BANK MANAGER

Banks may have lost much of their standing in the eyes of businesspeople but they nevertheless have what most companies need – money to lend. And so their quasi-monopoly of small business funding continues even though they are growing more expensive and more selective.

HOW DO THE CHANGES IN BANKING AFFECT THE MANAGER AND CUSTOMER?

There have been attempts to streamline business banking and bring together local business accounts. Though recently this policy too has been reversed with business account managers being put back into local branches. Companies with a turnover between £500 000 and £1 000 000 in the clearing banks are generally allocated to the small business manager. Each manager will control up to 500 accounts with the help of an assistant manager and say two senior clerks.

For the middle market, companies turning over in excess of £1m to £100m per annum the manager will have 40 to 60 customers or 'relationships'. Anecdotal evidence from the managers shows that for both markets only around two thirds of customers borrow. Banks offer around 200 services and products, from insurance to treasury products, which the manager is expected to promote to customers as appropriate. Factoring and invoice discounting are just two of these 200 products.

One problem facing the bank-owned factors is that bank managers, who are in a prime position to recommend their services, don't as often as perhaps would be appropriate because their time is at a premium with a large number of accounts to look after and a huge product portfolio to promote. The factors are competing for attention from the bank manager with the other bank group subsidiaries.

This is not the only reason for the continuing low market penetration that factoring and invoice discounting have achieved.

DO BANK MANAGERS UNDERSTAND FACTORING?

The banking text book, *Practice and Law of Banking* by Sheldon & Fidler, included a chapter on factoring for the first time in its eleventh edition in 1982. First published in 1920 it was left till 22 years after the arrival of factoring on these shores to include details of the services. This exemplifies the lack of importance attributed to factoring and invoice discounting by the banking profession even in relatively recent times.

Informing managers involved in the small business sector of services available within the group is largely done through the formal ongoing training run by the banks themselves. Subsidiaries also use their sales force to keep managers up to date and host open days to show managers how the systems work.

This raises awareness among bank managers of the in-house factoring services only. If competitors are mentioned at all it is likely to be those associated with other clearing banks. There would be no reason to mention the smaller independents as these do not represent a threat, as yet. Though we feel this will change over the next three to five years. Managers will therefore have a limited view of factoring services. This has been borne out by our research. Given the demands on the managers' time it is not surprising that the promotion of factoring is not a priority.

Due to the relatively low numbers of companies factoring or discounting, individual managers are unlikely to have had much experience of the service, its application, its benefits and weaknesses.

USING THE FACTOR AS RISK ASSESSOR

There is a growing recognition within some major banks that receivables financing is a skilled area in which subsidiary factoring companies may be able to help bank managers. This has led to bank managers becoming more aware of the specialist abilities of the factor.

There is also some doubt as to whether banks have the skills and systems to assess the risks inherent in lending against the sales ledger. The systems for monitoring the security (i.e. the book debt) are historical and usually based on monthly reports from the client. In reality this means a simple monthly statement by the customer of net current assets. As this takes some time to compile and submit, the bank manager can often be making lending decisions based on information which is two months old. The speedier submission of statements by the client to the bank would assist in more accurate lending.

This contrasts markedly with the security measures used by the factors, credit limits per debtor checked daily against sales and ongoing verification of debts. Even though the factors have tailor-made systems and specialist staff they themselves still suffer fraud and losses.

Banks generally set lending levels at between 30% and 50% of outstanding debtors, subject to an overall lending limit to a customer of 1:1, total net assets:total lending. We assumed that this was to allow for poor quality debtors, credit notes, debtor insolvency and any other causes that would weaken the security of the lender. Bank managers have been, however, unable to confirm any relationship between financing the sales ledger at 50% and risk assessments.

In-depth examination by the bank manager of the ledger prior to advancing funds against it is rare. If the client goes out of business and the bank needs to realise its investment from the sales ledger the process is not very effective – a central realisations department will liaise with the liquidator or receiver, who will then endeavour to collect funds due. The success rate of collecting outstanding debts to cover exposure is poor, we estimate this at around 80% by value.

Factors on the other hand have a much more secure exit route – they own the debts, debts can only be discharged by payment to the factor (whether the supplier is still trading or not), the factors have copies of all invoices and they have teams of professional collectors who can be brought in to accelerate the collection procedure. Our estimate is that where disclosed factoring facilities are concerned, factors collect out their exposure in full, in the event of a genuine client failures, in nine out of ten cases.

CHANGES IN ASSESSING RISK

Clearing banks are beginning to use skilled employees from their factoring divisions to assess the value of the debtor book asset where they feel the customer's financial stability is in question. The factoring surveyor will use standard factoring procedures to do this. With the help of their experience and dedicated systems this can be done efficiently and there is no need at this particular aspect to use the services of an investigating accountant.

On the positive side, managers have been known to call in a factor to assess whether the bank could prudently advance more funding against the ledger.

This recognition of these skills may eventually help the factors raise awareness of their services within the banks and in time win more business from their parent bank. It does, however, tend to promote the association between poor quality business and factoring, i.e. factors know what to look for when it comes to companies in financial difficulty.

Nevertheless, the acceptance by the bank that more specialised skills are needed to assess and manage funding of the sales ledger is borne out by the following recent development.

Currently on trial in the south of England, is a scheme whereby the clearer is using skilled credit managers to assess the appropriate lending levels to be advanced on a given ledger. These recommendations are then passed to the bank manager for consideration. Monitoring of the monthly statements is also conducted by the credit managers and recommendations are changed and updated accordingly. The scheme is designed to improve the bank's security and free the bank manager from administration chores.

BANK MANAGER AS PROFIT CENTRE

Bank managers are now individually targeted to generate income for the branch. A manager is unlikely to recommend the services of a subsidiary, even though they could be more suitable, if this means he or she will lose the income to be generated from lending. Thus we have a situation where the bank-owned factors who gain between 30% and 80% of their new business from the banks are being passed business only when it is deemed unsuitable for normal overdraft finance or term lending.

This means that companies who are stronger financially, who could nevertheless benefit from extra working capital and from sales ledger administration, may not be given the most suitable product to help them grow. There is no incentive for bank managers to recommend best quality customers to the factors. These are the customers that the factors would dearly like to add to their portfolios. Companies that could benefit from the extra working capital that factoring provides are not being given the option. The situation of generally not being passed best quality clients is compounded by the factors' lack of success in attracting these companies through other marketing methods.

BANK MANAGER AS TIED AGENT

Our research with bank managers has shown that they recommend, in 90% of cases, the in-house factor, if factoring is deemed applicable. Only if the factor is unable to write the business will a minority of managers recommend other factors, around 40%. When asked why they have never recommended a client to factoring or invoice discounting company NOT associated with the bank, two of the other 60% wrote, 'not company policy' and 'why should we?' Well, that is at least honest but it doesn't help the customer or the factoring industry.

WHAT DOES THIS MEAN FOR THE FACTORING INDUSTRY?

The bank manager behaves as any tied agent would, recommending his or her own company's products even though others might be more suitable. There is no incentive to find out about the merits of services provided externally. By passing leads to the in-house factor, fee and lending income are kept within the group. We have seen evidence of a bank manager insisting his client use the in-house factor instead of an independent factor, under threat of withdrawal of other bank facilities.

Increasingly, there is a tendency for factoring subsidiaries to pay a commission to bank branches which introduce clients. This can be done by paying cheques to the bank branch concerned or crediting the branch and manager with points or 'wooden dollars'.

Levels of commission paid for introductions vary by bank. Anecdote evidences that up to 20% of the first year's forecast fee income is payable. It has been suggested that there may be a correlation between the size of commission paid and market share – the higher the commission the greater the number of referrals – but we have not had confirmation of this from the factors and cannot confirm whether this is the case or whether any relationship between commission levels and referrals is causal.

No doubt any monies actually paid away by the factor will be taken into account when the shareholders (i.e. the Bank) look at the end-of-year figures and the return on capital employed.

Our research showed that many managers are actually unaware of commissions payable by their subsidiary factor.

EXAMPLE COMMISSION PAYMENT

A limited company, forecasting a turnover of £3 million was introduced by a bank manager to the in-house subsidiary. The factor agrees a service fee of 1% of turnover, finance charge of 3% over bank base rate with the customer and the customer factors its debts. Commission payable to the branch would be:

at 20% commission:

$$£3\ 000\ 000 \times 1\% \times 20\% = £6000$$

at 5% commission:

$$£3\ 000\ 000 \times 1\% \times 5\% = £1500.$$

IF OUR IN-HOUSE FACTOR CAN'T DO IT...

Another view expressed in interviews with bank managers was 'If our subsidiary would not factor the customer then no other company would', the assumption being that client selection criteria are the same throughout the industry. This is particularly worrying for the independent factors who offer between them services that cater for non-standard ledgers. As we have seen, bank managers are effectively 'tied agents', committed to selling the products of the banking group, hence if factoring is perceived to be needed by customers they will be referred automatically to the bank's own factoring house, regardless of the client's particular need.

As bank managers have access to an in-house provider of factoring services and are more or less obliged to use it, it removes the need for them to find out about other receivables financing services on the market. These key influencers are very often unaware that there are financiers who will look at: high concentration ledgers (where single debtor accounts for more than 20% of the ledger), factoring where the client is involved in collecting its own debts, certain industry sectors avoided by their own in-house factor, and providing higher finance levels against certain debtors.

One could say that the uninformed bank manager can potentially do more harm than good to factoring. The in-house factor may not be the best solution for the client's needs. Encouraging the customer to go along this route can result in dissatisfaction and may have contributed to giving the industry a poor name.

The increase in the number of factoring brokers whose role it is, among other things, to place business that has been rejected by one factor, is evidence of the diversity of services in the market. More than 90% of respondents estimated that there are 20 or more players in the market but only 10% could name factors that were not bank-owned. Ninety per cent also advised that if they needed information on the factoring market they would approach their subsidiaries.

Summary

Banks aren't charities and it is unrealistic to expect bank managers to behave indulgently to financially weak customers. Neither are they are impartial financial and business advisors and it can be expected that if a customer's requirement for factoring or invoice discounting is identified, the manager will recommend the services of the bank's own factoring subsidy. Customers must ascertain the benefits of these services and find out if there are other more suitable products available, with or without the manager's help. Free advice can be obtained from independent factoring brokers. Well-informed professional advisors may also be able to assist.

The clarification and acceptance of the position of banks and their managers are to be encouraged. Banks and their customers should be aware of the underlying motivation of the other.

Tips and traps – customers' guide

If you are interested in finding out the costs and benefits of using factoring or invoice discounting or your bank manager has recommended to you the services of the in-house factor check the following:

● How much commission does the manager or branch stand to make, or be credited with, if any, for recommending this service?

- How extensive is the manager's knowledge of the factoring market?
- Can she or he recommend any other factors?

If you decide to use the services of another factor will there be any difficulty in the manager giving a waiver to any existing charge over the company's debts?

Chapter 16

Factoring and professional advisors

Business advisors and accountants in particular are crucial to the future success of the factoring industry. The purpose of this chapter is to put forward possible reasons for the failure of the industry to win over significant numbers of accountants in practice. We have gained interesting insights into accountants' attitudes through interviews and discussions with The Institute of Chartered Accountants for England and Wales' General Practitioner Board which represents around 30 000 accountants.

Whichever factor is able to convince this influential group of advisors of the quality and validity of its services will be set to take a clear lead in the market. There is an opportunity here for a new major player, learning from the successes of others and delivering a high quality product, that is perceived as such, to dominate the market.

OVERVIEW

The services of factors and to a lesser extent discounters are most relevant to smaller companies. The typical traits of an average successful small business are:

- organic growth;
- few fixed assets against which to secure lending;
- lack of experience and systems to support good credit control;
- directors involved in debt chasing;
- no reserves to support bad debt losses or the long credit periods required by customers;
- undercapitalisation.

Factors can provide the assistance in all these areas: finance linked to sales not to fixed assets, optional bad debt protection, professional credit risk management and expert debt chasing, the latter usually resulting in an improvement in debtor days outstanding. However, as we have seen from the figures elsewhere in this book, market penetration remains extremely low. Why? We can assume that the benefits of factoring are just not getting through to decision makers in the UK's small companies.

Aubrey Selig, vice-chairman of the Association of Invoice Factors, puts this in perspective by pointing out that on average only two companies per bank branch factor, 15 000[1] out of a potential estimated market of 250 000. To try to assess why the message is 'not getting through' let us consider for a moment how a small business would reach a decision regarding its short- and medium-term funding requirements.

The importance of an advisor in influencing a buying decision

The owner-managed or owner-directed companies, firms in relatively early stages of development, do not generally have their own internal finance professional and would seek or expect to receive financial advice and guidance from external sources. Advice would most often come from perceived experts: accountants, financial or business consultants or the bank manager. No slur is intended by our using 'perceived' – we are trying only to make the point that many of the advisors listed are general practitioners and it is unlikely that any will be specialists in working capital finance and even more unlikely that any will have in-depth knowledge of the factoring industry itself. We have dealt in detail with bank managers in Chapter 15.

Ask the marketing manager of any factoring company what he or she would most want to achieve and the answer is likely to be, 'convert more accountants to the benefits of our services'. Accountants hold the key to greater use of factoring and invoice discounting because they have the ear of their small business clients. Hence the major financial influencers of opinion for this target market are accountants and other financial advisors.

Some accountants are aware of the potential benefits of the service in theory but few have experience of its successful operation for one of more of their clients. Mark Spofforth, Vice Chairman of the General Practitioners Board[2] agrees that 'The main advantage of factoring is that it enables you to grow borrowing in line with growing sales and this, to a large extent gets around over-trading, the main problem facing businesses as we come out of recession...'

Advisors produce the best leads

Interestingly the conversion rates of companies introduced to factoring by accountants and financial advisors that subsequently become factoring clients are generally around one in six to one in twelve, far outstripping conversion rates associated with direct marketing and advertising which can be as low as one in fifty (clients:enquiries). The one in twelve ratio will be considerably improved as the introducer becomes familiar with the selection criteria of the factors.

Good conversion rates show that business decisions such as choosing to factor one's debts are more effectively made as a result of advice from a respected business advisors. Hence the potential importance of the financial advisor to the factoring industry.

Commissions

Factoring companies will reward successful introducers of new business with commissions. These vary in size depending on the factor involved but are typically paid in one of three ways:

- percentage of first year's forecast fee income on commencement of factoring, can be 10%;
- percentage of the annual fee income for the first three years of the client's factoring facility, can be up to 7.5%;
- percentage of the annual fee income for the factoring life of the client, can be up to 7.5%.

These would be offered to accountants, brokers and other intermediaries, even existing clients who introduce a business. Many accountants will pass on the fee earned to the client. Mark Spofforth confirms that for members of the GPB the commissions are irrelevant to recommending or not recommending factoring as all commissions are passed on to their clients.

When taking advice from an intermediary it is as well for companies to ascertain the commission due to the advisor involved and any special relationship the introducer may have with the factor.

Factors are more than happy to pay commissions as this represents performance-related marketing. Leads that come from intermediary sources are mostly of a better quality than those generated directly from the market, being screened for suitability by the introducer and to an extent pre-sold, saving the factor time and marketing costs.

However the paying of commissions does not motivate accountants, a view confirmed by Mark Spofforth and many other accountants. This is likely to change as pressure on accountants' fees continues and other sources of income become more highly valued. Also as factoring and invoice discounting become more generally accepted and more widely used accountants may perceive the commission as a justified reward for researching the facilities or as a useful discount for clients.

Accountants are the key to market penetration

With small businesses, by their very nature, having to seek professional financial advice externally, practising accountants occupy a key position of influence. In our view the strength of their influence will increase as that of the bank manager continues to wane. Mark Spofforth echoes this opinion:

'The professional relationship that used to exist where the bank manager was your friend is now seen very much more in terms of the bank manager being there to make a profit for the bank.'

Apart from the damage done to the relationships between small businesses and bank managers caused by perceived high costs, over-charging and lack of lending authority, the banks will continue to be cautious with regard to the financing of small businesses. The small business looking for impartial advice on funding will probably turn to the accountant. Spofforth again·makes an interesting observation regarding the strength of the general practitioner accountant's relationship with the client, i.e. the practitioner will hold the client's hand through business law, tax, finance audit and also deal with the client's personal tax affairs, building up trust that he or she only gives impartial advice.

If the factors could positively influence accountants in larger numbers to the benefits of factoring, the effect on winning new small business clients would be enormous. Ironically however, it is the smaller independent factors who are making greater inroads rather than the major factors into the profession as explained below.

Other advisors

Apart from accountants there are other groups involved with providing professional expertise to small businesses: solicitors, management and financial consultants. All could be in a position to advise clients regarding financing and credit management. Solicitors are rarely targeted by the factors and it may be the case that marketing budgets are more effectively spent on other groups of intermediaries. Also over the last three or four years a large number of solicitors have started to offer clients debt collection services and are likely to view factors as competitors.

Commercial finance and general business consultants are a useful target for the industry. Often working as self-employed advisors, they are generally keenly motivated by the commissions to be earned by making introductions to a factor. They are usually engaged solely for the purpose of finding the solution to a particular problem or situation for the client rather than enjoying the general advisory status of the auditing accountant. Therefore they need funding solutions to put forward – factoring and invoice discounting are valuable additions to their products range. They are pleased to be able to offer alternative funding to the traditional bank overdraft.

Penetration of the business consultancy market has proved to be easier than that of the accountancy profession. It is becoming an increasingly important target for medium-sized factors with advertising in management consultancy journals more than doubling from 1993 to 1994.

Influencers of opinion

We should not overlook a group of non-fee-earning advisors also working with SMEs, such as the business counsellors at the Enterprise Agencies, the Chambers of Commerce and DTI soon to be merged into an organisation called Business Link. These agencies have been mostly ignored by the factoring and discounting companies. As these advisors have to be impartial and be seen to be impartial individual factoring companies may understandably feel they would make no direct gains from approaching them. However as an industry view this is at fault – all advisors if given the right information could put forward a more positive view of factoring. As it stands these sources of potentially positive influence remain with their generally held misconceptions of the industry unchallenged.

Specialist factoring brokers

At the time of writing (Summer 1994) there are a handful of brokers specialising in the placing of clients with factoring or discounting houses. The role they play is a useful one and can tie in naturally with accountants who do not have the time to become experts in the industry themselves. This could be particularly helpful to general practitioners. It also removes the problem of an accountant being seen to favour one factor over another, as long as the broker chosen to place the business is independent. Before referring to a factoring broker it is advisable to ensure that the broker is not tied to one or a few favoured factors, through special incentives or sponsorship. The emergence of specialist brokers is evidence of the growing diversity of services on offer.

Paul Samrah, partner at chartered accountants Kingston Smith, sums this up from the accountants' point of view:

> Now that the factoring and discounting market is maturing, the role of the broker is becoming more important. Professional advisors do not want to spend excessive time researching the market – this only involves clients in additional costs at a time when cash flow is, of course, not at its best...it is vital for that broker to be independent and to be seen to be independent.

ACCOUNTANTS IN PRACTICE

Factor: 'Do you ever recommend factoring to your clients?'
Accountant: 'No, it's too expensive.'
Factor: 'What are the average costs involved?'
Accountant: 'I don't know, but a partner in my firm dealt with a case about three years ago and I understand from him that it was expensive.'

The above is an excerpt from a conversation with an officer of a regional association of chartered accountants who is also a senior partner in an accountancy firm. This is just one example out of the many that we come across of the lack of current and precise knowledge of the services available.

Before we go any further we need to acknowledge that there are a small number of accountants who do recommend their clients to factoring and discounting. Research shows that this happens most often when the accountant already has a client who is factoring happily. However, what is unclear is whether subsequent recommendations to factoring are made as a positive first choice solution or only after other avenues have been exhausted. A partner in one London firm states that:

> Depending on the particular circumstances, I would not hesitate to recommend factoring and invoice discounting as a positive step forward in the cash management of a business. For a growing business, turning sales into a readily available source of funds is extremely important.

We are also aware of one body of accountants, The UK 200 Group, which has had informal relationships with factoring houses and will recommend their services when appropriate. This is evidence perhaps of a gradual improvement in attitudes towards factoring. However, in general the factoring option is not in our view given adequate and rational consideration by accountants.

Spofforth explains the accountants' stance: 'the product itself is perceived as being slightly dangerous, slightly risky'. It is safer not to get involved with it.

The theoretical benefits of factoring: more working capital and sales ledger administration are generally known among accountants but awareness is negated by misconceptions and fear of the untried and untested.

We feel that the reasons for continuing misconceptions and fear of factoring can be attributed more or less evenly to the complacency of the accountancy profession and the immaturity of the factoring industry.

Weaknesses in the accountancy profession

Lack of education

There is little or no formal instruction regarding factoring and invoice discounting within the accountants' professional exam curriculum. 'One of the modules in the second professional examination – the finals concentrated on methods of business finance, within which there was a single page on factoring and invoice discounting – explained the bare bones of the differences in services and that was all,' confirms Mark Spofforth.

Thereafter, during their continuing professional education (CPE) we noted the further absence of courses and instruction. This situation may have engendered the attitude in the profession that as factoring and discounting are not important enough to study, they are therefore not serious options in the world of business finance and credit management. Spofforth feels that the way to address this issue is for the factoring companies to provide training on CPE courses. He points out that this will enable general practitioners and others who specialise in business finance to gain current knowledge at the stage in their career when it is most relevant.

This leads us on to another problem area.

Which factor? Desire to be impartial and give best advice

'Ethics is very much in the press' said Jack Maurice, head of professional ethics at the Institute of Chartered Accountants.[3] Enquiries to the joint ethics committee of the accountancy bodies have risen to 1000 per month in 1994 from around 300 per month four years previously.

Accountants are required to be impartial and give best advice. Criticism of them is becoming more vociferous. With a generally imprecise knowledge of factoring they may well feel it is in keeping with their code of ethics to avoid this option entirely, even though the elements of the service would appear at first sight to offer solutions to a client's problems. By introducing a service of which they have had little or no experience do they fear doing more harm than good to the client? This is borne out by Spofforth's remarks on the perceived 'dangerous' nature of factoring and his view: 'This is partly because the practitioner CAN'T give best advice'.

Furthermore, even if the accountant agrees that factoring could be helpful to a specific client, which provider of services is he or she to recommend? Which would give the most appropriate facility? This requires detailed knowledge of the market, not just of the bank-owned factors. Accountants are generally aware of the major factors but would they recommend the factoring company belonging to a rival bank to where the client itself banks? Accountants may fear this will jeopardise existing banking relationships.

How can an accountant realistically give best advice in this specialist area? There is a modest but increasing trend whereby a handful of accountants are referring clients to specialist, independent factoring and discounting brokers whose role it is to source the most suitable facilities from the whole market.

Fixed ideas

Over the last two years the factoring industry has gained endorsement from industry leaders, Howard Davies, director general of the CBI, Eddie George, Governor of the Bank of England and Michael Heseltine, former President of the Board of Trade. This is one example of how factoring has improved its image with major influencers of opinion. But this positive attitude is not shared by many in the accountancy profession. The profession, conservative by nature, is lagging behind changes in opinions towards the factoring and invoice discounting industry.

Fear of loss of revenue

Do accountants fear a loss of revenue? Factors can take over the running of the sales ledger, advise on credit limits on new customers, automatically produce statements and accounts information. This information can be available on-line to the client as up-to-date as the close of business on the previous working day.

'This can remove the need for advice and management information accounting, previously carried out by accountants' is a view often expressed to us by people involved in selling factoring but vigorously denied by Mark Spofforth on behalf of practitioners.

Unfair and inaccurate comparison to overdraft finance

A cursory look at basic charges associated with factoring and with the bank overdraft would seem to indicate that the overdraft is cheaper. But this does not take into account the value-added nature of the factoring facility and the savings that can be achieved by users. As professional advisors it is reasonable to expect accountants to have analysed the market, the facilities, the costs and savings and the alternatives before giving an opinion. But this does not seem to be happening.

From our survey and those undertaken by the factors themselves into the attitudes of accountants, the major criticism levelled at factoring and discounting is 'it's too expensive'. This is, as the reader is probably well aware, 'an old chestnut' thus we have devoted Chapter 6 to an in-depth comparison of costs. Without wishing to analyse costs and savings at this particular juncture there are two principal points that should be borne in mind when considering whether factoring is expensive:

1. The factor is using its shareholders' funds to invest in a relatively high risk market (note the amount the banks lost in this market in the latest recession) for which it requires commensurate reward. The recent report sponsored by National Westminster Bank, 'The Future of Small Business Banking', confirms this. The banks appear to have miscalculated their risk/reward ratio for small business lending, leading to losses and tightening of customer selection criteria. It looks likely that charges will be increased to generate the right level of reward.
2. Expensive compared to what? Is there an alternative facility and will it provide the service that factoring or discounting gives?

Many small companies need more than working capital. Expert advice when selling on credit, assistance with the credit checking of customers, debt chasing and guaranteed cover against bad debts can be crucial to a company's survival. The associated charges can be less than the cost of employing one's own specialised staff to perform these tasks.

It would be certainly more accurate for accountants to ask 'Is the cost of the factoring administration fee higher than a company would normally pay for credit checking, collecting and credit insuring its own debts to an equally high standard?' and 'Is the cost of factoring finance higher than the cost of available overdraft funding and does the extra finance generally available from a factoring facility justify any difference there may be in charges?' True cost/benefit comparisons could do away with this criticism. For cost comparisons between factoring, invoice discounting and the bank overdraft, see Tables 6.2 and 6.3 in Chapter 6.

Factors' weaknesses – poor communication

The benefits of factoring are generally known by the accountancy profession but the profession's misconceptions, fears and valid criticisms are not being addressed. So market penetration is being hampered.

Unfortunately it appears that the factoring industry itself has done a poor job in allaying the fears of accountants. In our view it is the major factors who are largely at fault. Accountants and bank managers have commented on the poor quality of presentations given by the factors. Mail shots to accountants were also singled out for criticism. Seminars are frequently held by factors to communicate to mixed groups of accountants, bank managers and other advisors. We understand that the factors generally consider their seminars to be effective, however, Mark Spofforth disagrees:

> Where I have heard presentations from factoring companies they haven't frankly been very impressive. I think that perhaps they don't know the level at which to pitch the presentation or they don't know how best to get the message across.

The larger factoring companies determine general attitudes toward the industry

It is, in our view, significant that some of the independent factors derive up to 85% of their new business from introductions from accountants and other intermediaries. This information is based on recent interviews with directors and sales managers of several non-clearing bank owned factors. For the major factors it is the reverse, with up to 85% being introduced by the parent bank, and around 10% to 30% coming from other intermediaries, of which accountants are one. Scottish bank-owned factors are an exception – the scant bank branch coverage in England means other sources of referral had to be developed.

With a parent bank to hand passing on sufficient volumes of new business why should a factor spend significant time in addressing the misconceptions and reservations held by accountants? Furthermore if a significant number of new customers are available from the parent bank what is the incentive for the major factors to bring in new services or service enhancements? The result of the factor–bank relationship has meant that new services and product enhancements have not come about as quickly as they might have done in a truly competitive market. It would be difficult to say whether service levels have improved or not in the major factoring companies. Undoubtedly, more information is now available more quickly to the client.

When for the first time ever in the history of the ABF&D the volume of members' clients' factored turnover fell in 1991, marketing and sales strategies were overhauled. Given that the average time a client stays with one factoring company is between two to four years, problems contributing to a fall in turnover would have been in existence in the late 1980s. Here are some possible causes for the fall in the number of companies using factoring:

- As the recession took hold higher risk customers in particular were passed from the bank to the factors, some of these then failed while with the factor.
- The factors had enjoyed the boom years, with new clients clamouring for finance for growth being referred to them by the banks. This type of client now faded away.
- There were no sales or marketing initiatives directed at alternative sources in place, to supplement the fall in introductions from the bank.

Since this time there has been a general tightening of selection criteria before a client is taken on by the factors, meaning that companies with the same profile which may have been accepted four years earlier are now being rejected.

The major factors have also sought to reduce their reliance on a single source of business and to begin work on winning over other potential introducers of business and are focusing more efforts towards the accountancy profession.

Evidence of this is the amount of advertising by the factors in the accountancy press and the employment of executives targeted only with building relationships with accountancy firms, working alongside the direct sales force.

In short due to the cushioning effect of the parent bank, the major factors have only latterly recognised the importance of a marketing-led culture, where the customer is number one, criticisms are addressed consistently and clearly and professionals are dealt with professionally.

Smaller factors compete on quality of service

Independent factors operate in a truly competitive environment. They make up around 10% of the market by volume and gain most of their clients through introductions from advisors. Between them they have developed some very flexible domestic factoring services, for example where clients are involved in collecting their own debts or there is a high concentration of sales to one customer and niche products to suit situations like CVAs considered 'unfactorable' by others.

An example of high service levels achieved by this part of the industry is provided by Maddox Factoring, with a modest 110 clients. Maddox work in a cell system. The small teams that look after the clients get to know them. 'Each debt, even if it's only £5 is chased by telephone' says Pat Munday, director. 'The big factors rely on computer generated dunning (chasing) letters. We don't think this is the best way because customers get used to the system and wait for the last reminder. These small sums can mount up. We are selling a service and clients appreciate the personal touch and attention to detail.'

Quality of service

As explained above there was until recent years little need for bank-owned factors to adapt services to meet the varying needs of clients. Nevertheless the products in their basic form still had many benefits for customers. Technological advances were brought about to facilitate the handling of increasing numbers of clients and paperwork, with a by-product being greater efficiency and hence better client service.

Some of the very large factors have been likened to 'sausage machines' – a reference to their supposed slavish adherence to computer-set risk parameters and client management based on exception reporting rather than understanding of the needs of individual clients. With the major factors there is a perceived lack of individually-tailored services and flexibility. This perception is largely shared by accountants and therefore the argument that factoring in general is a value-added service is weakened. To pay for overheads – staff, premises and computer systems – the major factors need to generate high volumes of business. In a high-volume business individual tailoring of products to meet specific needs may suffer. However, there are thousands of companies which find these service levels quite acceptable.

As with their parent banks, factors are using more technology and will continue to reduce staff numbers relative to client numbers. The eventual benefit of this could be significantly lower prices for their clients. The image of a relevant, quality service has yet to be communicated by the major factors to accountants in general.

Decision makers Quality of service is linked also to the decision-making powers of the individuals responsible for the day-to-day running of the client's account. If, as in many large organisations, the management structure is hierarchical, the decision-making chain for non-standard situations can be long. The result is often that the client can be left waiting for answers to questions crucial to the running of his/her business.

Only one of the major factors has moved away from the large processing departments to a 'cell' structure. This is a fairly forward thinking move as initial processing efficiency could be reduced but the quality of service can be increased. The function of the cell system is briefly this: a collector, credit assessor, data input clerk and one client liaison executive will work in a team together dealing with say 100 to 200 clients.

Members of the team will become familiar with the aspects of the clients' business in relation to their factoring facility and decisions can be made by the client executive based on up-to-the-minute feedback from the other members of the team. This approximates the existing structure within the smaller factoring companies.

If the bigger factors want to increase market penetration significantly they must give the quality and flexibility of service that companies want. Between the smaller players in the market this flexibility already exists. Smaller factors do not have the financial resources to make radical advances in large-scale conversion of accountants. However, if strategically the majors see their future as primarily a service to the parent bank then the size of the factoring market will depend on the banks' small business lending policy, rather than the factors' ability to meet customers' diverse needs (Chapter 15).

If service levels are improved and costs are acceptable accountants may be more disposed to recommending the services of the major factors to their clients.

Quality of personnel 'in-house'

The major factors have grown their businesses with a large number of clerical staff. As years have gone by managers and staff have been promoted to increasingly senior positions, leading to very efficient processing departments. Many senior managers and directors have had real experience of risks and systems that make up their business.

The skills and expertise of major factors to successfully provide receivables financing services are not in doubt. What is in doubt is whether they can successfully market their products outside their respective banking groups? So far, judging from the non-conversion of accountants in any significant number, they have failed. Apart from lack of orientation towards client needs it is our view that the general absence of professionally-qualified sales and senior staff within the majors has contributed to the negative attitude held by most accountants towards the industry.

We looked at the sales forces of several factors and invoice discounters and found many of the larger ones have no professionally qualified individuals.

One medium-sized factor, which generates 80% of its business from non-bank introductory sources, has a sales team made up of professionally-qualified personnel, chartered accountants and associates of the Chartered Institute of Banking. Another very small but successful factoring company's directors are all chartered accountants. Bank of Ireland Commercial Finance Limited in Dublin employs around 60 people of whom six are chartered accountants and several others ACIB.

Many of the smaller factors can field better professionally-qualified sales-people, managers and directors than the majors. This is by no means suggesting that this will affect the efficiency of their services but it could be significant when trying to influence professionals such as accountants. Accountants tell us they prefer to work with other professionals. By employing more of them the major factors could help overcome the accountants' fear of what they perceive to be a 'risky product'.

A hard sell approach will not win over accountants, rather it can only serve to reinforce the negative attitudes that accountants have.

Failure to address (perceived) faults

One area to be addressed is the collection of debts by the factors without upsetting the relationship between the client and customers. The worry of bringing in a factor who will alienate a client's customers is one which is frequently voiced by accountants. Whether this is a real or perceived risk is not the issue. The fact that it persists with accountants limits the growth in the market. The view needs to be addressed head-on and challenged in a consistent and convincing way. Criticisms need to be met openly and if mistakes have been made they must be acknowledged.

Accountants do not want to be sold to, they prefer to buy.

Hamstrung by the banks

If the factors who are subsidiaries of the clearing banks were able to achieve greater market penetration it would be to the benefit of the whole industry, increasing awareness of the service and its benefits with end users and intermediaries.

It can be argued that the major factors and invoice discounters are prevented from achieving greater success by their parent banks. The bank overdraft is factoring's biggest and probably only competitor, but direct comparisons on price cannot be made in the factors' marketing campaigns or material because their parent bank would not allow it. On average, more than 50% of new clients come from the parent bank. High cost is so often cited by accountants for not factoring that it is lamentable when accurate cost comparisons cannot be made at every opportunity.

All significant marketing initiatives are subject to approval by the banks' own marketing departments. Hence factors cannot openly meet head-on, the main criticism that accountants level at their service.

Comparison between the bank overdraft and invoice discounting could be especially useful in addressing criticisms.

Credit to the smaller players

The independents have no parent banks on whom to rely for a large proportion of their introductions. Yet even during the recession they managed to achieve an increase in client turnover. In 1991 the body representing nine of the independent factors, the Association of Invoice Factors, recorded an increase in clients' turnover of 14.5%. The ABF&D members recorded a fall in factoring turnover.

Interestingly the smaller discounters and factors do not have the sizeable marketing budgets available to the bigger players in the market with which to promote their services directly to the potential client. So their success is all the more marked. The independents have by necessity had to gain the confidence of accountants and other financial advisors who are their main sources of referral.

Summary

We foresee no large-scale conversion of accountants until the perceptions relating to cost, service levels and quality communications have been addressed. Because of the involvement of the banks in the market the cost issue is unlikely to be clarified. A gradual improvement in the views will, however, come mainly from the efforts of the independent factors and a growing familiarity with factoring in general.

To bring about significant changes in the perceptions that accountants have of factoring one of three things would need to happen:

1. The largest and therefore most influential factors would need to complete their transition from sales-led to marketing-led organisations where customer satisfaction exceeds in importance adherence to rigid parameters, where highly-trained staff ensure prompt responses to non-standard situations while adequately managing risk and those representing the company are suitably qualified.
2. Banks will change lending policies so radically (possibly due to their previous enormous losses in this sector) that many small businesses are either unable to get bank finance or finance will be 'too expensive'. Factoring will become the main source of receivables financing, thus more or less forcing accountants to take note and to give it the credibility it deserves.
3. A major new player will enter the industry, possibly a foreign bank.

NOTES

1 ABF&D – Companies using ABF&D members' services in 1993 were 10 092, Association of Invoice Factors members had 764 clients in 1993 and we estimate a maximum of 750 clients spread among the other factors and discounters in the UK.
2 The GPB is the body of the ICAEW which represents the smaller general accountancy practice specialising in services for companies turning over up to £2.5 million and employing less than 50 people.
3 *The Independent* 16/8/94.

Chapter 17

The new bankers

There is a tide in the affairs of men which, taken at the flood...

And so it is with the factoring and invoice discounting industry. The coming two years could see the greatest flourishing of the sector if the opportunity is seized. Never before have the economic conditions coincided to create such a favourable environment. The industry could become the new bankers to British industry.

The factors and discounters could be set to take over the role traditionally undertaken by high street bankers in terms of commercial financiers. They have the skills, systems and experience to provide 250 000 small- and medium-sized UK businesses (SMEs) with the finance and support they need during the economic upturn. 250 000 is our estimate of the number of firms who stand to benefit from and are eligible for factoring or invoice discounting. Bank managers have shown they do not have the skills needed now and are rightly reluctant to lend where they are unable to manage the inherent risks.

In simplified terms the lending expertise of bank managers has been linked to property – the current economic upturn is not underpinned by a rise in property values. How can they provide the working capital that companies need?

But will the major players, the clearing-bank-owned factors make the most of this? Or will a new player from the UK or overseas enter the market at this ideal time and snatch this opportunity away?

We foresee a continuing expansion in the market regardless of any changes in strategy existing factors might implement or the entry of any new, major parties. This expansion will as before be largely driven by the demand for unsecured finance – that is funding which is not linked to fixed assets such as property and equipment. However, growth could be greatly accelerated by astute action by a sizeable organisation.

THE WINDOW OF OPPORTUNITY

UK banks have been subject to enormous criticism regarding their treatment of small businesses, some undoubtedly justified. However, attitudes to banks and bank managers have changed – it has become apparent that many of today's managers have not been sympathetic to or even understood the needs of their small business clients. Client–manager relationships are now more firmly based on commercial realism rather than vague notions of avuncular indulgence.

Factoring companies have come out of the recession unscathed by such criticisms. The disenchantment within the business community should strengthen the factors' hand – more companies will be open to considering other forms of finance.

Nevertheless people's memories are short and interest rates are now the lowest they have been for many years. Both will help diminish any bad feelings towards the banking sector. The factoring industry will need to move fast and purposefully.

THE FACTORING MARKET

There are around 60 companies in the market which is dominated by the major clearing-bank-owned factors. Although the smaller factors have been responsible for more product innovation and flexibility of service it is only a major player that would have the capability to effect a radical increase in market penetration in the short term.

The industry is still young, 35 years in the UK, but there is already considerable product differentiation especially among the smaller factors. Specialist brokers have emerged to service companies looking for facilities from this diverse market.

IMAGE AND QUALITY SERVICE

Factors have gone some way to change the 'finance of last resort' image but their success remains hampered. There are two main causes – misconceptions held by financial advisors and other businesspeople and shortcomings in some of the factors' services and in their marketing. Underpinning this is the semi-dependence of many of the major factors on their parent bank for new clients, with over half their new business coming from this source. This confusing relationship – in a normal market the bank with its overdraft product would simply be a competitor – has contributed to the lack of innovation and development in the market.

A FAVOURABLE ENVIRONMENT

Property – no longer 'as safe as houses'

The fall in property values and the losses experienced by the banks who thought their funding had been secured by a charge over property assets has called into question the extent to which fixed assets really can 'secure' loans.

The sales ledger – a powerful asset

As a result many more small- and medium-sized businesses will find that the sales ledger has become the most powerful asset for attracting finance. Companies will want to maximise finance against this asset. Banks don't have the systems to manage financing against this type of security, factors and discounters are expert in it.

THE BANK MANAGER – SALES MANAGER

The traditional bank manager's lending skills are related primarily to property. Levels of financing could be calculated relatively easily and hands on monitoring was not needed. Will they be retrained to lend against the sales ledger? Will they be given the systems with which to manage and monitor such lending? This would call for massive investment when the banks have over recent years tried to reduce overheads.

Today's bank managers are also responsible for the retailing of around 200 bank products – they have become general practitioners and salespeople rather than specialists. Conversely the factor and discounter have in-depth expertise of one area only and are not (at the moment) selling any other services. However, some are looking at services which could bolt on to the core factoring and discounting facilities. This will further enhance their standing as the new bankers.

WHAT BUSINESSES WANT

Even though some of the criticism of the banks has been unfair, most people were genuinely shocked by the way the banks reacted to a difficult trading period. The repayment 'on demand' condition of the overdraft and loan agreement was seen enforced with dramatic consequences.

Finance was withdrawn or refused, contributing not only to company failure but to company directors losing family homes put up as loan security. The subsequent break up of marriages and families made poignant reading in the press. This has focused the minds of those who need to raise finance for business on keeping personal assets separate from the business.

The effect of this would be to remove another property asset against which bank managers have traditionally had experience of lending and will reduce the fixed assets at the disposal of the small business against which to raise finance – making full use of the sales ledger asset even more important.

Discounters and factors link their finance to the sales ledger and if they wish to terminate an agreement have to give notice of anything up to six months. Also they generally seek to recover their exposure from collecting monies due against factored invoices.[1]

Directors may no longer view 'cost' as more important than security in assessing financing facilities. This could help the factoring industry overcome the general criticism of the perceived high costs of its services.

COMPANIES NEED TO STAY LEAN

Costs have been cut in order for companies to compete and survive in the recession. Companies actively sought out areas of unnecessary cost and pruned them, leading to many painful management decisions to shed staff. Those areas that were most visible have been addressed. Two things may result from this in the favour of the factor:

1. The cost of financing slow payers has become more visible now that other cost areas have been addressed.
2. Employers are reluctant to take on staff permanently to run the sales ledger and other functions when company growth may be uncertain.

The value-added service of factoring could address both these areas. Factors can generally reduce debtor days outstanding by their efficient collection services. Also a factor's collection services can be used instead of employing staff when workloads cannot be assured.

GEARING

With profit margins being squeezed companies will need to sell more to maintain levels of profit. Banks are hooked in to gearing as a means of calculating the amount of funding they can safely provide. Gearing is the value of net assets compared to the amount of borrowing made by a company.

Property values are lower but more working capital is needed to fund the higher level of sales required to generate profits. Financing as a function of net assets will increase. Gearing is not a formula used by the factors and where used by invoice discounters ratios are around 250–300% (compared to the banks' typical 100%).

WHO WILL SEIZE THE OPPORTUNITY?

The factors and discounters have the right products for the current and foreseeable economic environment for many businesses. What could stop them from capitalising on the opportunity? The smaller ones will continue to do well but the largest organisations who could make a significant difference may fail the industry as a whole. We should remember that they don't need to change to survive in the short term, when this major opportunity is there – the parent bank will presumably keep feeding them business.

The increase in turnover during the 1980s of around 20%[2] annually appears to have allowed the majors to survive without innovating or focusing on standards of delivery. Production and sales-led attitudes to new business have not changed. Their introspection is evidenced by the introduction of their own industry educational qualifications, rather than promoting qualifications which are already recognised by the all important external bodies in accounting and credit management.

Will it be easier for a new player – one that does not have the above mentioned encumbrances – to step in and build on the work already done?

THE VIEW OF THE FINANCIAL ADVISORS

Accountants and other business advisors are important in the financial decision-making processes of SMEs which has obvious implications for the factors and discounters. Although research has shown that the workings of factoring and discounting are understood by most accountants and advisors, they seldom recommend these services. Objections and criticisms of the services are centred round a perceived high cost and loss of control of the sales ledger. Whether these criticisms are well-founded or not – they are discussed in Chapter 16 – they must be addressed and changed by the industry to effect any large expansion in the market.

Having said that, to what extent are professional advisors responsible for keeping themselves advised of services available? We have found that misconceptions exist among many accountants and there is little knowledge of the diversity of facilities on offer. Are those that base opinions on anecdote and rumour really fulfilling their duty of care to the client? A proper understanding of these financing facilities would enable a rational and valid recommendation to be made to business clients. Clients expect best advice.

THE UK NEEDS THE NEW BANKERS

Our economy is growing. Growth is largely from SMEs who need working capital to fund expanding order books. Where will this working capital come from? In general terms it will not be available from the banks. The 'old bankers' have skills relating to property and fixed asset lending. Properties have fallen in value and are no longer viewed as rock solid security.

The sales ledger has become an even greater part of the total assets of a company. It is now this asset that must be used to secure finance. The 'new bankers', the factors and discounters, have the skills learnt over the last 35 years to provide the appropriate finance and services. The levels of receivables financing that the factors can make available will not be accessible from the bank overdraft.

Understanding receivables financing is what the discounters and factors do best, it is their specialism. There have been recent promising developments into stock financing from some factors. So far this has been used for higher-quality customers and bolted onto factoring or invoice discounting facilities. It increases working capital available without reliance on fixed assets and is another step towards displacing the traditional bank funding. The trend has again come from the USA and could represent the beginning of a major enhancement to factoring and invoice discounting. The UK factoring industry has developed computer systems to manage its involvement with small businesses. The industry's staff are expert in assessing the sales ledger for financing purposes and in the case of factors are skilled at controlling the associated risks through debt chasing and credit management.

Through the new bankers many of the companies that we rely on to generate economic prosperity can access the finance required and improve their chances of success.

NOTES

1   Termination due to suspected client fraud would of course be managed differently.
2   Take into account the booming economy, inflation at 5% from 1984 to 1993 and increases in the number of factors in the Association.

Glossary – the jargon buster

Administration charge Charges made by the factor/discounter for administering the facility, expressed as a percentage of a company's gross turnover.

Advance rate The agreed level of finance advanced against approved invoices. (*See also* Initial advance.)

Ageing Monthly report showing the age of invoices outstanding.

Agency factoring The provision of factoring finance, with the client collecting monies, acting as the 'agent' for the factoring company.

Approved debt A debt against which the factor agrees to advance monies.

Assignment stamp Details on an invoice which confirm that the debt has been assigned to the factoring company.

Associate company A company linked with the client by common directorship or shareholding.

Availability The amount of funds available to a client at any given time.

Bad debt protection Protection offered by a factor in the event of an approved customer becoming insolvent, providing the debts remain undisputed.

Bootstrap buyout Where only borrowed funds using the assets of a target company are used to acquire a company.

Bulk factoring *See* Agency factoring.

Commercial recourse factor Smaller factoring company which provides recourse factoring (q.v.) without setting finance limits.

Commission *See* Administration charge.

Confidential factoring An alternative expression for confidential invoice discounting or undisclosed factoring.

Confidential invoice discounting The provision of sales-linked finance, where the client runs their own sales ledger and the customers are not aware of the factor's involvement.

Correspondent factor An overseas factor who co-operates with the domestic factor by offering credit control and management services in the respective overseas country.

Credit approval The provision of bad debt protection (q.v.) against a given customer.

Credit approved debt A debt which has been given credit approval.

Credit limit The limit given to a client in respect of a customer.

Debt turn Average number of days for outstanding invoices to be collected.

Disclosed invoice discounting Confidential invoice discounting (q.v.) where the client's customers are aware of the factor's involvement via an assignment stamp (q.v.) on the invoices.

Discounting charge The cost of money advanced to a client charged by a factor. Similar to bank interest rates and expressed as a percentage over bank base rates.

Dispute The client's customer refusal to accept the merchantability of goods or services.

Export factor The factoring company in the country where a client company is undertaking business. The export factor liaises with the domestic factor to provide a collections and underwriting service to the client.

Exposure *See* Funds in use.

Factoring The backbone of the industry, providing the three basic elements of the service – finance, credit control and sales ledger administration.

Finance charge *See* Discounting charge.

Finance limit A limit set against a client's given customer, which reflects the amount of finance that will be advanced against a given customer's invoices.

Funds in use The total level of funds advanced to a client – the factor's level of exposure.

Import factor A factor who provides services in relation to debtors in his or her own country for a client in another either directly or through an export factor.

Ineligible debt Debt which the factor does not consider for funding purposes, generally because of the age of the debt.

Initial advance/prepayment The funds released on day one of a factoring or invoice discounting facility commencing.

Interest *See* Discounting charge.

LBO Leveraged buyout – using only borrowed funds to effect a management buyout.

Letter of offer Formal offer of facilities to a client.

Margin The proportion of invoices which automatically remain unfinanced – i.e. if the prepayment facility was 80% of approved invoices, there is an automatic margin of 20%.

MBI Management buyin – where a management team external to an existing company seek to buy out the company.

MBO Management buyout.

Merchant financing The provision of finance, where the goods themselves are technically sold to the financier. The financier then advances an early payment to the client, once the goods have been accepted by the client's customers.

Non-recourse factoring Factoring (q.v.) where the client has the additional benefit of bad debt protection (q.v.).

Prepayment *See* Advance rate, Initial advance.

Receivable Debt to be sold to the factor by the client. Normally any debt arising in the normal course of the client's business.

Recourse factoring The provision of factoring without the benefit of bad debt protection. With any old debts (usually over 90 days past due) the debts are reassigned to the client.

Refactoring charge An additional charge levied by some recourse factors in the event of debts assigned to the factor ageing beyond an agreed limit – usually 90 days past due.

Reserve *See* Retention.

Retention The amount of any invoices assigned to the factor which are unfinanced. (*See* Margin.)

Service charge *See* Administration charge.

Take on/take-over debts Debts in existence at the commencement of factoring.

Unapproved debt A debt which the factor does not approve for funding purposes owing to a lack of creditworthiness.

Appendix

Members of the Association of British Factors and Discounters (ABF&D)

	Parent company	Address	Telephone number
International Factors Ltd	Lloyds Bank plc	PO Box 240, Sovereign House, Church St, Brighton, E. Sussex BN1 3WX	01273 321211
Lombard Natwest Commercial Services Ltd	National Westminster Bank Group	Smith House, PO Box 50, Elmwood Ave, Feltham, Middlesex, TW13 7QD	0181-890-1390
Griffin Factors Ltd	Midland Bank plc	21, Farncombe Rd, Worthing, West Sussex, BN11 2BW	01903 205181
Alex Lawrie Factors Ltd	Lloyds Bank plc	Beaumont House, Beaumont Rd, Banbury, Oxfordshire, OX16 7RN	01295 272272
TSB Commercial Finance Ltd	TSB Group plc	Boston House, The Little Green, Richmond, Surrey, TW9 1QE	0181-940-4646
Barclays Commercial Services Ltd	Barclays Bank plc	Aquila House, Breeds Place, Hastings, East Sussex, TN34 3DG	01424 430824
Royal Bank Invoice Finance Ltd	The Royal Bank of Scotland plc	Exchange Court, 3, Bedford Park, Croydon, Surrey, CR0 2AQ	0181-686-9988

	Parent company	Address	Telephone number
Trade Indemnity–Heller Commercial Finance Ltd	Trade Indemnity Group plc/Heller Europe Ltd	Park House, 22, Park St, Croydon, Surrey, CR9 1RD	0181-681-2641
Kellock Ltd	Bank of Scotland	Abbey Gardens, 4, Abbey St, Reading, Berkshire, RG1 3BA	01734-585511
UCB Discounting Ltd	Groupe Paribas	UCB House, 36–60 Sutton Court Rd, Sutton, Surrey, SM1 4WS	0181-401-4000
Close Invoice Finance Ltd	Close Brothers Group plc	Southbrook House, 25, Bartholemew St, Newbury, Berkshire, RG14 5LL	01635 31517
Venture Factors Ltd	ABN AMRO Holdings N.V.	Sussex House, Perrymount Rd, Haywards Heath, West Sussex, RH16 1DN	01444 441717

Members of the Association of Invoice Factors (AIF)

	Address	Telephone number
Anpal Finance Ltd	P.O. Box 37, Kimberley House, Vaughan Way, Leicester, LE1 9AZ	0116-251-6066
Bibby Factors Ltd	Kenwood House, 77A Shenley Rd, Borehamwood, Herts, WD6 1AG	0181-207-1554
Bibby Financial Services Ltd	105, Duke Street, Liverpool, L1 5JQ	0151-708-8000
Gaelic Invoice Factors Ltd	Finlay House, 10–14 West Nile St, Glasgow, G1 2PP	0141-248-4901

	Address	Telephone number
KCH Ltd	The Computer Centre, Benmhor, Campbeltown, Argyll, P28 6DN	01586 554488
Maddox Factoring (UK) Ltd	Argent House, 1, Progress Business Centre, Whittle Parkway, Slough, Berkshire, SL1 6DQ	01628 668706
Metropolitan Factors Ltd	33, Boltro Rd, Haywards Heath, West Sussex, RH16 1BL	01444 415081
RDM Factors Ltd	Fairfax House, 461–465 North End Road, London, SW6 1NZ	0171-386-7233
Ulster Factors Ltd	7, North St, Belfast, BT1 1NH	01232 324522

Members of the Commercial Finance Association – European Chapter

	Parent company	Address	Telephone number
AIB Commercial Services Ltd, Dublin	Allied Irish Bank plc	Balls Bridge, Dublin 4.	010 353 6600311
Barclays Commercial Services Ltd	Barclays Bank plc	Aquila House, Breeds Place, Hastings, East Sussex, TN34 3DG	01424 430824
BI Commercial Finance Ltd	Bank of Ireland	Alhambra House, 9, St. Michaels Rd, Croydon, Surrey, CR0 2RA	0181-686-0900
Bank of Ireland Commercial Finance Ltd, Dublin	Bank of Ireland	Lower Baggot St, Dublin 2	010 353 1 6689777
Bank of Ireland Corporate International	Bank of Ireland	Donegall House, 7, Donegall Square North, Belfast, BT1 5LU	0232 246241

	Parent company	Address	Telephone number
Causeway Invoice Discounting Co. Ltd	Causeway Capital 40% ECI Ventures 40%	12 St Ann's Square, Manchester, M2 7HS	0161-832-4442
Close Invoice Finance Ltd	Close Brothers Group plc	Southbrook House, 25, Bartholemew St, Newbury, Berkshire, RG14 5LL	01635 31517
Heller Europe Ltd	The Fuji Bank Ltd	4, Millbank, London, SW1P 3JA	0171-973-0033
ITT Commercial Finance Ltd	ITT Corporation	Unit 2, Woking 8, Forsyth Rd, Woking, Surrey, GU21 5SB	01483 727788
National Bank of Canada	National Bank of Canada	Princes House, 95, Gresham St, London, EC2V 7LU	0171-726-6581
Singer & Friedlander Commercial Finance Ltd	Singer & Friedlander Ltd	41–43 Maddox St, New Bishopsgate, London, W1R 0BS	0171-499-6343
Trade Indemnity–Heller Commercial Finance Ltd	Trade Indemnity Group 50% Heller Europe Ltd 50%	Park House 22, Park St, Croydon, Surrey, CR9 1RD	0181-681-2641
Transamerica Commercial Finance Ltd	Transamerica Corporation	Centre 3, Wilbury Way, Hitchin, Herts, SG4 0TP	01462 420442
TSB Commercial Finance Ltd	TSB Group plc	Boston House, The Little Green, Richmond, Surrey, TW9 1QE	0181-940-4646
UCB Invoice Discounting Ltd	Group Paribus	UCB House, 36–60 Sutton Court Rd, Sutton, Surrey, SM1 4WS	0181-401-4000
Venture Factors plc	ABN Amro Holdings N.V.	Sussex House, Perrymount Rd, Haywards Heath, West Sussex, RH16 1DN	01444 441717

Unaffiliated factoring companies and invoice discounting houses

	Address	Telephone number
Alexanders Commercial Finance Ltd	CL Woodchester House, Selsdon Way, London, E14 9GL	0171-987-0838
BI Commercial Finance Ltd	Alhambra House, 9, St. Michaels Rd, Croydon, Surrey, CR0 2RA	0181-686-0900
Causeway Invoice Discounting	12, St. Anne's Square, Manchester, M2 7HS	0161- 832-4442
Cl Woodchester Trade Finance Ltd	CL Woodchester House, Selsdon Way, London, E14 9GL	0171-538-9300
County Factors Ltd	26, Hill St, Poole, Dorset, BH15 1YL	01202 680934
De Lage Landen Invoice Factors Ltd	PO Box 215, Westcombe House, 2–4 Mount Ephraim, Tunbridge Wells, Kent, TN4 8ZZ	01892 703500
Herebond Ltd	St Mary Abchurch House, 123, Cannon Street, London, EC4N 5DR	0171-623-9446
Isis Factors Ltd	Wolsley Court, Station Rd, Goring-on-Thames, Reading, Berks, RG8 9HE	01491 875660
Northern Bank Factors Ltd	PO Box 533, Harvester House, 4–8 Adelaide St, Belfast, BT2 8GA	01232 326655
Osbourne Best Factors Ltd	63/65 High St, Skipton, North Yorkshire, BD23 1EF	01756 799511

	Address	Telephone number
Portland Factors Ltd	115, Eastbourne Mews, London, W2 6LQ	0171-402-7890
Reedham Factors Ltd	Richmond House, 15, Bloom St, Manchester, M60 7PP	0161-237-1483
Silverburn Finance Ltd	6, Winter Hay Lane, Horwich, Bolton, BL6 7NZ	01204 669666
Singer & Friedlander Factors Ltd	21 New Street, Bishopsgate, London EC2M 4HR	0171-621-0006
Sygnet Management Services Ltd	10 Thornton Park Avenue, Muxton, Telford, Shropshire TF2 8RF	01952 676328
TSB Factors Ltd	Mountshill House, 141–154, Brent St, London, NW4 2DW	0181-203-9909
Ulster Bank Commercial Services Ltd	11 Donegal Square South, Belfast BT1 5PH	01232 438388

Merchant financiers

	Address	Telephone number
Fairfax Gerrad Ltd	Fairfax House, 461–465 North End Road, London SW6 1NZ	0171-386-7233
Foster Church Merchant Trading Company Ltd	161, Newhall St, Birmingham, B3 1SW	0121-236-1457
RegalBrook Ltd	P.O. Box 6, Holywood, County Down, BT18 0JB	01232 428151
Stenham plc (merchant finance division)	34, John Street, London, WC1N 2EU	0171-831-0551

	Address	Telephone number
Trade Indemnity–Heller Commercial Finance Ltd (Merchant Finance Division)	Park House, 22, Park St, Croydon, Surrey, CR9 1RD	0181-681-2641
Versailles Trade Finance Ltd	Bechtel House, 245, Hammersmith Rd, London, W6 8DP	0181-528-9868

Other useful addresses

	Address	Telephone number
The Association of British Factors and Discounters	1, Northumberland Avenue, London, WC2N 5BW	0171-930-9112
The Association Of Invoice Factors	c/o Gaelic Factors Ltd Finlay House, 10–14 West Nile St, Glasgow, G1 2PP	0141-248-4901
Chartered Association of Certified Accountants	29, Lincolns Inn Fields, London, WC2A 3EE	0171-242-6855
DTI	General Enquiries	0171-215-5000
Institute of Chartered Accountants	Chartered Accountants Hall, Moorgate Place, London, EC2P 2BJ	0171-920-8100
Institute of Credit Management	The Water Mill, Station Road, S. Luffenham, Oakham, Leics. LE15 8NB	01780 721888
Institute of Export	64, Clifton St, London, EC2A 4HB	0171-247-9812

Specialist factoring and invoice discounting brokers

	Address	Telephone number
Cashflow Solutions Ltd	95, Ditchling Rd, Brighton, East Sussex, BN1 4ST	01273 692567

Figure A1   Factors Chain International

MEMBERS OF FACTORS CHAIN INTERNATIONAL

FCI Secretariat, Keizersgracht 559, 1017 DR Amsterdam, The Netherlands
Telephone +31-20-6270306 Fax +31-20-6257628 Telex 11261

Country	Members	City	Principal shareholders
Australia	Scottish Pacific Business Finance Pty Ltd	Sydney	Bank of Scotland
Austria	Intermarket Factoring AG	Vienna	GZS-Unternehmensbeteiligungs AG GKI-Holding Gesellschaft m.b.H. Österreichische Kreditversicherungs AG Steiermärkische Bank und Sparkassen AG
	VB-Heller Bank Aktiengesellschaft	Salzburg	Österr. Volksbanken Aktiengesellschaft Heller International Group, Inc.
Belgium	ACE Factors S.A./N.V.	Brussels	ASLK - CGER Bank
	Belgo-Factors N.V.	Turnhout	General Bank Heller International Group, Inc.
	CERA Factors N.V.	Leuven	CERA Bank
Canada	Accord Business Credit Inc.	Toronto	Wholly-owned subsidiary of Accord Financial Corp., a publicly quoted co.
China	Bank of China	Beijing	The Government
	Bank of Communications	Shanghai	The Government
Colombia	Banco Colpatria S.A.	Bogota	Capitalizadora Colpatria S.A. Constructora Colpatria S.A.
Cyprus	Bank of Cyprus (Factors) Ltd.	Nicosia	Bank of Cyprus Ltd.
	Laiki Factors Ltd.	Nicosia	The Cyprus Popular Bank Ltd.
Czech Republic	O.B. Heller A.S.	Prague	VB Heller AG Československá Obchodni banka, a.s. International Finance Corporation
	Transfinance Ltd.	Prague	Transakta Zivnostenská banka Ltd. Intermarket Factoring AG Bayerische HypothekenBank AG Factofrance Heller
Denmark	Forenede Factors A/S	Copenhagen	Den Danske Bank A/S
	Nordisk Factoring A/S	Copenhagen	A/S Jyske Bank Heller International Group, Inc.
Finland	Finnish Customer Finance Ltd.	Helsinki	Union Bank of Finland Ltd.
France	BNP Factor S.A.	Paris	Banque Nationale de Paris (B.N.P.)

Country	Members	City	Principal shareholders
	Banque Sofirec	Paris	The Edmond de Rothschild Group Public Compagnie de Suez
	Factofrance Heller	Paris	Heller International Group, Inc.
	Factorem	Paris	Caisse Centrale des Banques Populaires Other Banques Populaires
Germany	Deutsche Factoring Bank	Bremen	Bayerische, Bremer and Hamburg-ische Landesbank, Landesbank Hessen-Thüringen, Landesbank Rheinland-Pfalz, Landesbank Schleswig-Holstein, Norddeutsche and Westdeutsche Landesbank
	Disko Factoring Bank GmbH	Düsseldorf	Dresdner Bank AG Hermes Beteiligungen GmbH
	GEFA Gesellschaft für Absatzfinanzierung mbH	Wuppertal	Deutsche Bank AG
Hong Kong	OTB International Factors Ltd.	Hong Kong	Overseas Trust Bank, Ltd.
	The Hong Kong and Shanghai Banking Corporation Ltd.	Hong Kong	HSBC Holdings Plc
Hungary	Hungarian Foreign Trade Bank Ltd	Budapest	Hungarian Ministry of Finance and other enterprises
	Magyar Factor KFT.	Budapest	Magyar Hitel Bank Rt. Intermarket Factoring AG
	Postbank and Savings Bank Corp.	Budapest	State, Hungarian Post Co., Österreichische Postsparkasse and other business organisations
Iceland	Landsbanki Íslands (The National Bank of Iceland)	Reykjavík	Republic of Iceland
India	fIntegrated Finance Company Ltd.	Madras	Privately held company
	SBI Factors & Commercial Services Pvt. Ltd.	Bombay	State Bank of India, Union Bank of India, State Bank of Saurashtra, State Bank of Indore, Small Industries Development Bank of India
Indonesia	Pt. BII Finance Centre	Jakarta	Bank Internasional Indonesia
	Pt Salindo Perdana Finance	Jakarta	Bank Dagang Negara (State Bank)
Italy	Barclays Factoring S.p.A.	Milan	Barclays Bank plc
	C.B.I. Factor S.p.A.	Milan	Istituto Centrale di Banche e Banchieri together with 72 other private banks

Country	Members	City	Principal shareholders
	Centro Factoring S.p.A.	Florence	Casse di Risparmio Firenze, Centro Leasing S.p.A., Banco di Sardegna and some 70 other Casse di Risparmio
	COFIRI Factor S.p.A.	Rome	COFIRI S.p.A. 61%, Ilva S.p.A. 5%, Banca di Roma S.p.A. 10%, Iritecna S.p.A. 5%, STET S.p.A. 5%, Alitalia S.p.A. 5%, SME S.p.A. 4%, Finmeccanica S.p.A. 5%
	Factorit S.p.A.	Milan	31.5% Banca Popolare di Novara 20% Banca Popolare di Milano Balance among 75 Italian Popular Banks
	Istituto Bancario San Paolo di Torino S.p.A.	Milan	76% San Paolo Bank Holding S.p.A. 24% public
	Mediofactoring S.p.A.	Milan	70% Cassa di Risparmio Delle Provincie Lombarde, 30% Banco di Sicilia
	Montepaschi Factor S.p.A.	Turin	Gruppo Monte dei Paschi di Siena
Japan	Dai-ichi Kangin Factoring Co., Ltd	Tokyo	The Dai-Ichi Kangyo Bank, Ltd.
	Diamond Factors Ltd.	Tokyo	The Mitsubishi Bank, Ltd. and others
	Sumigin General Finance Co., Ltd	Tokyo	The Sumitomo Bank, Ltd. and others
	The Central Factors, Ltd.	Nagoya	The Tokai Bank Ltd and others
	The Hyogin Factors, Ltd.	Kobe	The Hyogo Bank, Ltd.
Korea	Central Investment & Finance Corp.	Seoul	The Dongkuk Group and others
	Cho Hung Bank	Seoul	Korea Life Insurance Ltd. and others
	Dong-A Investment and Finance Corp.	Seoul	Daelim Industrial Co. and others
	Industrial Bank of Korea	Seoul	The Government
	Jaeil Investment and Finance Corp.	Seoul	K.H. Shin and others
	Pusan Investment & Finance Corp.	Pusan	The Lucky-Goldstar Group and others
	Sam Hee Investment and Finance Corp.	Seoul	Hanwha Group
	Shinhan Investment & Finance Corp.	Seoul	Korea First Bank
	The Commercial Bank of Korea, Ltd.	Seoul	Public Bank

Country	Members	City	Principal shareholders
Malaysia	Arab-Malaysian Merchant Bank Berhad	Kuala Lumpur	AMMB Holdings Berhad
	MBf Factors Sdn Bhd	Kuala Lumpur	MBf Leasing Sdn Bhd
Mexico	Banamex Factoraje, S.A. DE C.V.	Mexico	Grupo Financiero Banamex Accival. S.A.
	Factoraje Bancomer, S.A. DE C.V.	Mexico	Bancomer, S.A.
	Factoraje Serfin, S.A.	Mexico	Grupo Financiero Serfin General Electric Capital
	Factor Quadrum de Mexico, S.A. DE C.V.	Mexico	Servicios Financieros Quadrum, S.A.
Morocco	Banque Commerciale du Maroc	Casablanca	Sociéte financière DIWAN (groupe ONA), a number of Insurance companies, and others
	Wafabank	Casablanca	Private Moroccan Group Indosuez – Paris
Netherlands	De Lage Landen Factors B.V.	Eindhoven	De Lage Landen International BV (wholly owned by Rabobank Nederland)
	FMN Factoring	's-Hertogen-bosch	VSB Group N.V.
Norway	Elcon Finans A/S	Oslo	Gjensidige Group
	Factonor A.S.	Ålesund	Client companies, Investment companies, Banks
	Factoring Finans AS	Oslo	Den norske Bank
	Uni Storebrand Factoring AS	Ålesund	UNI Storebrand Finans AS
Portugal	BNP Factor, S.A.	Porto	Banque Nationale de Paris Group Union des Assurances de Paris
Romania	Romanian Bank for Development, S.A.	Bucharest	Romanian State
Singapore	DBS Factors Pte Ltd.	Singapore	The Development Bank of Singapore Ltd.
	Keppel Factors Pte Ltd.	Singapore	K Investment Holdings Pte Ltd
	OUB Factors Pte Ltd.	Singapore	Overseas Union Bank Ltd. Overseas Union Trust Ltd.
	Singapore Finance Ltd.	Singapore	Hong Leong Finance Ltd.
Slovakia	VUB Factoring	Bratislava	Všeobecná Úverová Banka Slovenská Záručná Banka Ibea Ltd.
South Africa	Nedbank Commercial Services Ltd.	Johannes-burg	Nedcor Bank Limited
Spain	Bansabadell Factoring, S.A.	Sabadell (Barcelona)	Banco de Sabadell S.A.

Country	Members	City	Principal shareholders
	Catalana de Factoring	Barcelona	Banca Catalana
	Heller Factoring Española, S.A.	Barcelona	Banco Popular Español Heller Holding France S.A.
	Hispafactor, S.A.	Madrid	Corporación Financiera Hispamer (Banco Central Hispanoamericano)
	Santander de Factoring, S.A.	Madrid	Banco de Santander, S.A.
Sweden	Handelsbanken Finans AB	Stockholm	Svenska Handelsbanken
Taiwan (R.O.C)	CITC Co., Ltd.	Taipei	CITC Investment Co., Ltd. China Leasing Company, Ltd. Others
Thailand	Siam General Factoring Co., Ltd.	Bangkok	Siam Commercial Bank Ltd. Group GF Holdings Co., Ltd.
Turkey	Aktif Finans Factoring Hizmetleri A.Ş.	Istanbul	Vakifbank Group, GSD Foreign Trade, Türk Eximbank, Garanti Bank, Finansbank Group, Public
	Devir Factoring Hizmetleri A.Ş.	Istanbul	Private Turkish Investors
	Euro Factoring Alacak Alimi A.Ş.	Istanbul	Compagnie Financiere de Camondo, Elia Eskinazi, Marmara Bankasi, and others
	Factofinans Alacak Alimi A.Ş.	Istanbul	Iktisat Finansal Kiralama A.Ş. Avrupa ve Amerika Holding A.Ş.
	Heller Factoring A.Ş.	Istanbul	Heller International Group, Inc. International Finance Corporation Yapi ve Kredi Bankasi A.Ş. Interbank A.Ş.
	ÍS Factoring Finansman. Hizmetleri A.Ş.	Istanbul	Türkiye Is Bankasi A.Ş. and others
	Türkiye Kalkinma Bankasi A.Ş. Development Bank of Turkey	Ankara	State owned bank
United Kingdom	Alex Lawrie Factors Ltd.	Banbury	Lloyds Bank plc
	Barclays Commercial Services Ltd.	Hastings	Barclays Bank plc
	Chancery Factors Ltd.	London	Chancery plc
	Griffin Factors Ltd.	Worthing	Midland Bank plc
	Kellock Ltd.	Reading	Bank of Scotland
USA	BNY Financial Corporation	New York	The Bank of New York
	NationsBank Commercial Corporation	Atlanta, Ga	NationsBank
	Rosenthal & Rosenthal, Inc.	New York	Rosenthal Inc.
	The CIT Group/Commercial Services Trust Company Bank	New York Atlanta	60% Dai-Ichi Kangyo Bank Ltd 40% Manufacturers Hanover Corp. SunTrust Banks, Inc.

THE INTERNATIONAL FACTORS GROUP

AUSTRIA Factor Bank, GmbH, Vienna
BELGIUM International Factors S.A., Brussels
BELGIUM Credit Lyonnais Eurofactors S.A., Brussels
DENMARK Unifactoring A/S., Copenhagen
DENMARK Bikuben Finans A/S., Copenhagen
FRANCE Société Francaise de Factoring International Factors France S.A., Paris
FRANCE Société Lyonnaise d'Affacturage S.A., Paris
GERMANY DG Diskontbank AG., Frankfurt
GERMANY Credit Lyonnais Factoring GmbH, Munich
HONG KONG OTB International Factors Ltd., Hong Kong
HUNGARY Merkantil Bank, Budapest
HUNGARY Central-European International Bank Ltd., Budapest
IRELAND International Factors (Ireland) Ltd., Dublin
ITALY International Factors Italia SpA, Milan
ITALY Credit Factoring International SpA, Milan
JAPAN Sanwa Factors Ltd., Tokyo
KOREA Republic of Daihan Investment & Finance Corporation, Seoul
KOREA Republic of Bando Investment & Finance Corporation, Seoul
KOREA Republic of Samsan Investment & Finance Corporation, Seoul
MEXICO Factoring Comermex SA de CV, Mexico City
MOROCCO Maroc Factoring, Casablanca
NETHERLANDS International Factors Nederland BV., Rotterdam
† **NORWAY** Factoring Finans, Oslo
PORTUGAL International Factors Portugal S.A., Lisbon
SINGAPORE International Factors (Singapore) Ltd., Singapore
SPAIN B.B. Factoring S.A., Madrid
SPAIN Banesto Factoring S.A., Madrid
SPAIN International Factors Espanola S.A., Madrid
SPAIN Credit Lyonnais Iberica de Factoring S.A., Madrid
† **SWEDEN** Svenska Finans AB., Stockholm
SWITZERLAND Factors AG., Zurich
TURKEY Aktif Finans Factoring Hizmetleri AS., Istanbul
UNITED KINGDOM International Factors Ltd., Brighton
UNITED STATES OF AMERICA BancBoston Financial Company, Boston
UNITED STATES OF AMERICA Republic Factors Corporation, New York

†Partner

Index

Page references in **bold** refer to figures and page references in *italic* refer to tables.